EDEXCEL GCSE POETRY ANTHOLOGY

COLLECTION B: CONFLICT

CONTENTS

About the Author 2
About this Guide 3
THE POEMS 15
A Poison Tree – William Blake 17
The Destruction of Sennacherib – Lord Byron 21
Extract from *"The Prelude"* – William Wordsworth 25
The Man he Killed – Thomas Hardy 31
Cousin Kate – Christian Rossetti 35
Half-caste – John Agard 41
Exposure – Wilfred Owen 45
The Charge of the Light Brigade - Alfred, Lord Tennyson 53
Catrin – Gillian Clarke 60
War Photographer – Carole Satyamurti 64
Belfast Confetti – Ciaran Carson 70
The Class Game – Mary Casey 74
Poppies – Jane Weir 79
No Problem – Benjamin Zephaniah 86
What Were They Like? – Denise Levertov 90
Links, Connections, Comparisons & Tackling the Unseen Poem 95
A Note on Metre 103

About the Author

After graduating from Oxford University with a degree in English Language and Literature, and 26 years working for British Airways, I decided to train as a teacher of English. For the next ten years, I taught in the secondary state sector in a multi-cultural and socio-economically diverse area west of London. On my retirement in 2016, I was second in the English department, co-ordinator of the A Level English Literature curriculum and Lead Year 13 tutor, co-ordinating university entrance applications. I am also an Examiner for AQA GCSE English Literature.

My approach to studying poetry is straightforward: unless you understand *what is happening* in the poem – the event, incident or story – about which the poet weaves his literary magic, there can be no understanding of a poet's literary techniques. The two are inextricably intertwined. There is a LOT of very variable analyses of poetry on the internet. Much of it stems from a failure to understand *what is happening*. This failure leads to students having a rattle-bag of literary terminology but with nothing on which to hang it. Naming metric forms and rhyme schemes, and poetic techniques, with no understanding of why the poet has used them, is a waste of time. It also leads to spurious, and erroneous, analyses of structure and form. I have read, in exam papers, that the *"shape of the line on the page, if you turn it sideways, corresponds to the furrows of a field."* Or, *"the varied line length suggests the outline of the Manhattan skyline"*. Students do not come up with ideas like this unless there is a fundamental failure to grasp the links between *substance (*the *"what is happening")* and *structure (*rhythm and rhyme*)* and *language (*the words used*)*.

This guide is an attempt to make these links and help students appreciate why a poem has been written in the way that it has

About this Guide

The Guide has been written primarily for students of GCSE English Literature as specified by EDEXCEL in the post-2015 syllabus (1ET0). It addresses the requirement to study one cluster of poems taken from the *EDEXCEL/Pearson Poetry Anthology* and the requirement to analyse and compare two Unseen poems. These requirements are assessed in Component 2 (19th century Novel and Poetry since 1789), Section B: Poetry, and Section C: Unseen Poetry, of the examination.

The Guide aims to address Assessment Objectives AO1, AO2 and AO3 for the examination of this component, namely:

AO1: Read, understand and respond to texts. Students should be able to:
- maintain a critical style and develop an informed personal response
- use textual references, including quotations, to support and illustrate interpretations. *[1]

---

[1] *Whilst there is no specific mention of *"making comparisons"*, the mark scheme makes it clear that the examiners expect the essay response to be *"comparative"*, described as *"Critical, exploratory comparison"* at the highest band.

AO2: Analyse the language, form and structure used by a writer to create meanings and effects, using relevant subject terminology where appropriate.

AO3: Show understanding of the relationships between texts and the contexts in which they were written.

The poems are explored individually, with links and connections between them drawn as appropriate. The format of each exploration is similar:

- An explanation of key features of the poem that require contextual knowledge or illustration and the relationship between the text and its context.
- A summary of the key themes of the poems, with a note on possible thematic links to other poems in the cluster
- A brief summary of the metric form, rhyme scheme or other structural features, related to the theme
- A "walk-through" (or explication) of the poem, ensuring that what is happening in the poem is understood, how the rhythm and rhyme contribute to meaning, an explanation of the meaning of words which may be unfamiliar, an exploration of language and imagery and a comment on main themes.

A note on "themes" (AO1 task)

The question (or *task*) in the examination for *Component 2 (19th century Novel and Poetry since 1789), Section B: Poetry,* will be on a theme which may form the focus of the poem or be an integral part of its meaning. You will be asked to make a comparative exploration of the presentation of this *"theme"* in one named poem and one other poem of your choice from the collection.

Section C: Unseen Poetry will ask you to explore the presentation of a given *"theme"* in an Unseen poem and compare it to the treatment of the same *theme* in a second Unseen poem.

Given that Collection B: is titled *"Conflict"*, you can expect to be asked to explore various ideas and perspectives on this theme. This could include, but not be limited to, the various kinds of *conflict* presented in the Collection, as between nations, in wars, between parents and children, or lovers, or individuals, or between sections of society or between man and nature. It could ask for an exploration of a relevant **emotion** – such as anger, loss, sorrow, envy; the **evocation of "place"**, as the subject of the poem, or as the setting for the poem; the treatment of **abstract concepts** such as Time, Power, Death, Conflict or Religion; a **"happening"** such as War, Childhood, Death, Emigration; types of **relationships between men and women,** such as unsatisfactory, jealous, obsessive, changing. The range is very broad.

Where a poem from the anthology lends itself to suggesting a particular theme, this has been noted in the overview and linked to other poems which have similar themes. However, these suggestions are illustrative, not exhaustive; one of the skills to be mastered is to know the texts well enough to be able to link them to themes which may not be immediately obvious. Students should spend some time mapping the links between poems thematically and illustrating how these themes are treated in similar or differing ways.

As well as links of *theme,* links and connections should be made between *narrative voice, form, structure* and *language.* At the end of this book are some questions which should be considered when making links and connections, and when analysing the Unseen (see *"Links and Connections."*)

A note on "relevant subject terminology" (AO1)

This means the *semantic field* of literary criticism, or "jargon". Criticism has a language to describe the features peculiar to the study of literature, just as football has words to describe manoeuvres and equipment – *"penalty", "off-side", "wing", "long cross", "throw-in".* To be able to critique literature, you need to know this language and use it correctly. Throughout this guide, literary terminology has been *italicised,* indicating that these words need to become part of your vocabulary when discussing the texts and writing essays. For illustration, here are some very basic literary terms that are often carelessly used and will make your writing in exams less effective if you do not apply them correctly.

Text – is the printed words. The *whole text* is all the words that are identified, usually by a *title*, as belonging together as an integral piece of writing.

A *book* is a collection of printed pages bound together to make a *whole text*. A *book* can be any text – fiction, non-fiction; play, novel; car maintenance manual, encyclopaedia. A *book* is a **physical** entity, like *"DVD"* or *"scroll"*, not a creative one.

A *novel* is a particular kind of text – a *genre*. It is characterised by certain creative features, such as being *fictional,* usually *narrative in structure* and with various *characters* who do things, or have things happen to them. It may be *descriptive* and may contain *dialogue*. A *novella* is a short novel. Its scope and the number of characters are often (but not always) more limited than in a novel.

A *short story* is a narrative fiction, of variable, but limited length.

A *play* is another *genre*. It is designed to be performed and watched, rather than read. It can be *fictional* or *non-fictional*, or a mixture. It is predominantly made up of *dialogue* between *characters*, although there may be descriptive elements within this *dialogue* and in the *stage directions*.

A *poem* is a particular *genre* which is characterised by the deliberate, and recurring, use of *rhythm* and *rhyme* and/or by a particular attention to *diction*, in the form of *word-choice* and *imagery*. It is opposed to *prose*. However, there are *poetical* prose writers whose language uses the distinctive features of poetry – such as *alliteration*, *rhythm* and *imagery*.

Beyond these simple definitions, there are a host of other literary terms. These terms have been used where they are necessary to describe features of the texts and are defined on the first usage, and subsequently when repeated, depending on how common the usage and the relevance to the poem under discussion.

There is a trend towards teaching students grammatical terms – such as the parts of speech – and using these in essays, in the mistaken belief that these will gain marks under use of *"subject terminology"*. This achieves very little. The feedback from the Examining Boards make it clear that linguistic analyses, including analysis of parts of speech, have little merit when demonstrating *critical understanding*. It is also better to avoid using subject terminology if you are unsure of its exact meaning.

A note on "critical comparisons" (AO1)

The new specification refers to *"links and connections"* as well as *"comparisons"* between literary texts. There is little to be gained from making, often spurious, comparisons which fail to illuminate the text, and structuring essays which say *"on the one hand/ on the other"*. The highest band marks challenge the student to be able to *synthesise* their knowledge of the texts – a higher level skill. The Mark Scheme refers to: *"critical, exploratory, well-structured comparison"*. Further guidance on this is given in the section on *"Links and Connections"*.

A note on "create meanings and effects" (AO2)

There are very few marks to be gained by simply spotting and correctly naming literary techniques. Even fewer if those terms are used incorrectly. It is better NOT to use a literary term at all than use the wrong one. **NEVER build an essay around literary techniques; you need to focus your essay on the thematic question (the "*task*"), showing how form, language and structure contribute to meaning.** Comments on literary techniques **must** be linked to purpose and meaning to gain marks in the higher bands. This principle has been followed in the analyses of the texts. Not all literary techniques used by the poets are discussed in the commentaries; only those that are particularly relevant to the discussion of meaning, form or theme have been explored.

You are also required to know something about *metric form* – the use of rhythm and the terms which are used to describe it – and relate the use of *metre* to meaning. Metre has been explained in the commentaries. Stressed beats are in **bold** and the *metric feet* are shown with the / symbol. *"A Note on Metre"* has been given at the end of this guide, which explains the main metric forms used, with examples from the texts.

Finally, you need to know when form and structure are used *for effect* and when the choice of a form or structure is part of a poetic tradition or a feature of a poetic movement (e.g. *Romantic, Modern*). Sometimes poets write in sonnet form because they like writing sonnets; they are following a tradition; it was expected by their readers at the time of writing. Similarly, with choices of metre. Both *iambic pentametre* and *ballad form* (alternating lines of *iambic tetrametre* and *iambic trimetre*) are common metric forms used by very many poets of different eras because it was a common form for poetry. It *may* be valid to link the choice of metric form to the poet's theme and it *may* be that the poet uses the metric form within the poem for effect. However, making far-fetched and spurious connections between choice of form and theme are largely a waste of time. Sometimes a *sonnet* is just a *sonnet*. However, *how* (rather than *why*) the sonnet form is used in a poem should be explored. For example, where the *volta* occurs, the use of rhyme and the use of rhyming couplets, and these choices related to meaning.

A note on "relationship between texts and context" (AO3)

There is a requirement to have some knowledge of the biographical, social-economic, political or literary context in which these poems were written **and show how this is reflected in the text.** "Context" is also taken to mean *"ideas and perspectives"*. This may include understanding the relationship between the specific themes of the poem and the more general attitudes of society at the time. Edexcel has given further guidance:

- the author's own life and individual situation, including the place and time of writing, only where these relate to the text
- the historical setting, time and location of the text
- social and cultural contexts (e.g., attitudes in society; expectations of different cultural groups)
- the literary context of the text, for example, literary movements or genres
- the way in which texts are received and engaged with by different audiences, at different times (for example, how a text may be read differently in the twenty-first century from when it was written).

Understanding of meaning is enriched by knowing relevant autobiographical details, particularly where the subject matter focuses on relationships. Many poems use allusions and references to classical mythology, the Bible, popular culture and general **knowledge**, without which meaning is obscure and appreciation limited.

Relevant contextual information has been given for each poem in either the introduction under "**Context**" or in the analyses.

A note on *typography*

Typography is the way the words of the poems are printed on the page. Remember – most poems, until relatively recently, were written by hand and therefore the look of a poem on the page when it is printed is not necessarily an indication of intent by the poet – it may be the *typography*. There are conventions in *typography* for poems which are adhered to by certain editions but ignored in others. For example, many of the pre-1900 poems start each line with a capital letter. This is of no significance – it is a typographical choice. Similarly, whether lines are indented or blocked may be typographical, rather than meaningful. Similarly, line length is often a feature of *metre*. Check that a line is, in fact, "longer" metrically before commenting on it. You should always look for other, supporting, evidence if you are going to make any link between layout on the page and meaning.

Capitalisation of individual words in a poem may be deliberate. Pre-1900 poets often capitalised virtues, as in Truth, Beauty, Purity or Nature. You should be able to tell whether capitalisation is a printing convention, or for a purpose, from the context. Where this is critical to understanding, it has been mentioned in the commentaries.

You will see in the older poems that the final *"-ed"* of the past tense of verbs may be depicted as *"'d"*, as in *"Volley'd and thunder'd"* in *"The Charge of the Light Brigade"*. This is simply to indicate that the words should be pronounced as two syllables. Sometimes, to make a full metric line, they would have been pronounced as three: *"thun-de-red"*. Alternatively, words which are usually pronounced as a single syllable were sometimes elongated to two, to complete a metric line. This was indicated by an accent symbol above the second syllable. However, this does not appear to have been standardised in the Collection. So, in *"A Poison Tree"*, line 7 should have an accent on "*sunned*", as it would have been pronounced "*sun-néd*" to complete the metric line: **And** I/**sun**-*néd*/**it** with/smiles.

Preparing for the Unseen Poems

The best preparation for this component of the examination is to read, and listen to, poetry of all kinds, regularly. There are websites which will deliver a "*poem-a-day*" to your mobile. These two combine contemporary American poetry with classics:
https://www.poets.org/poetsorg/poem-day
https://www.poetryfoundation.org/newsletter
The Poetry Foundation website enables you to browse poems clustered by theme. This is a particularly useful feature to enable you to practise comparing poems.

How to use this Guide

As the modern poems within the anthology are copyrighted to the authors, it has not been possible to print them within this Guide. You will therefore need to read the commentaries with a copy of the text alongside. However, the poems have been quoted in places for illustrative purposes. Where the poems are out of copyright, they have been quoted at greater length.

Bibliography

Edexcel have published supporting materials for the Collection which are available to teachers.

Further reading on context can be found on the following useful websites:

http://www.bl.uk/romantics-and-victorians/articles/the-romantics#

The British Library has a number of articles in their Discovery section on modern literature.

www.victorianweb.org

Many of the modern poets have their own websites, which are worth exploring for autobiographical details and commentaries on their poems.

THE POEMS

A Poison Tree – William Blake

Context

Like other Romantic poets (Blake, Wordsworth, Byron, Coleridge, Keats and Shelley), Blake challenges the supremacy of rational, scientific thought, seeking for spirituality and the transforming power of the imagination in human lives. He was a visionary and mystic, as well as a painter and engraver. He was considered "dangerous" for his expression of ideas that challenged conventional norms. The poem *"The Poison Tree"* is taken from the collection *"Songs of Experience"* (1794), a counterpart to *"Songs of Innocence"* (1789), which Blake describes on the cover of the combined volume as *"the two contrary states of the human soul"*. Childhood, for the Romantics, was a time of innocence, unconstrained by the conventions of society and the stifling authority of Church and State. *"Experience"* is the exposure to these corrupting influences, against which Blake protests. All the poems were illustrated by Blake in the original publication. The illustration for *"A Poison Tree"*, held in the British Library, can be seen on the Wikipedia entry for the poem.

Themes

Many of Blake's poems are *allegories* which, in telling a story, give a moral message. In this poem, Blake explores **the corrupting power of anger** on the individual's psyche through the *extended metaphor* of an apple tree that bears a poison fruit which eventually slays his former friend. Blake is warning against nurturing negative and vengeful thoughts, which destroy relationships, rather than embracing the concept of forgiveness. It is likely that both friend and foe in the first stanza are the same person, but perceived differently, depending on whether the speaker chooses to tell his friend how he feels, or keep his resentment hidden, thereby turning friend into foe.

The poem can be linked thematically to Hardy's *"The Man He Killed"* which also shows how perceptions of others can be twisted by negative thoughts. In Hardy's poem, soldiers are trained to see a stranger as an enemy in time of war, although there is no personal animosity between them. In Rossetti's *"Cousin Kate"*, close friends become enemies when courted by the same man. **Expressions of anger** are also found in Agard's, Casey's and Zephaniah's poems, where the anger is directed against a society which stereotypes them.

Form, structure and language

Like Hardy, Blake uses a regular pattern of rhyme and rhythm which acts as a counterpoint to the theme. The poem is one of Blake's *"Songs"*, written in *quatrains*[2] of *rhyming couplets*. The rhythm is a combination of *iambic tetrametre*[3] and *trochaic tetrametre catalectic*[4].

---

[2] *Quatrains* are stanzas of four lines
[3] Lines of four *iambs* - light/**heavy** or ti-**TUM**
[4] A *trochee* is the opposite of an *iamb* – **HEAVY**/light or **TUM**-ti. A *catalectic* line is one with a missing foot at the beginning or end. See the Note on Metre for a fuller explanation.

This metre gives the poem the sing-song rhythm of nursery rhymes and is a favourite structure of Blake's. Here, as in other *Songs,* the child-like innocence of the structure is at odds with the deadly subject matter. For comparison, Agard, Casey and Zephaniah all use rhythm to emphasise strong negative emotions.

In **stanza one**, two possible responses to being angry are presented, the *anaphora*[5] of "*I was angry*" setting them as equal, but opposite. The first response to anger is to make one's feelings known and "clear the air", which leads to a positive outcome; the second is to bury the anger and allow resentment to grow, poisoning the relationship and creating a perceived enemy. The lines alternate between *trochaic tetrametre catalectic* (or *headless iambic tetrametre*) and *iambic tetrametre*, as if he has not yet made up his mind which course to take.

In **stanza two**, the rhythm settles into the more insistent *trochaic tetrametre catalectic*, as his anger grows. Blake shows how the hidden resentment is nurtured by his fear of speaking out and by his frustrated *"tears"*. The repeated *"And"*, creating a *syndetic list,*[6] shows the care with which he builds his deceitful *persona,* piece by piece. On the outside, he presents a cheerful and smiling face, likened to the sun

---

[5] *Anaphora* is the repetition of the opening words of a sentence or phrase
[6] A *syndetic list* is one created using *"And"*. A list created with commas is called *"asyndetic"*.

shining on a growing plant (the metaphor for his anger), whilst he deceitfully hides his true feelings.

Stanza three extends the metaphor and sees the fruits of his nurturing. His anger is transformed, outwardly, into an attractive and positive appearance, an *"apple bright"*, which, we can infer, is like his original, cheerful disposition before his anger took hold, which "shines" out, as if beckoning his friend to come close. Lulled into a feeling of false security, his former friend approaches and embraces him as before. The use of natural imagery here can be compared with the image of the caged birds in *"Cousin Kate"* to represent the two women.

Blake's religiosity and moral purpose are evident in **stanza four** in the image of the apple tree, as in the Garden of Eden, the speaker being the serpent. Seduced by the outward show, the former friend approaches. The word *"stole"* is suggestive of deceit, and the *"veil'd…pole"* (pole, or North, star) tells us that it is under cover of darkness. Both images are a projection by the speaker of his own twisted mind, making foe of friend and attributing evil intent where none exists. He is triumphant in his "victory" over his *"foe"*, who has been vanquished by the full force of his anger and lies dead at the foot of *"the poison tree"*. Note how the final line is stretched out, like his foe, into a full *iambic pentametre* line.

20

The Destruction of Sennacherib – Lord Byron

Context

George Gordon Byron, 6th Baron Byron, was notorious for his love-life. He was described by one of his early mistresses, Lady Caroline Lamb, as *"mad, bad and dangerous to know"*. He was the archetype of the *Byronic hero*, a sexually alluring but dangerous, brooding and essentially ego-centric male protagonist who recurs through much of later Victorian fiction, including Rochester in *"Jane Eyre"* and Heathcliff in *"Wuthering Heights"* by the Brontes. Perhaps less well-known is that he was also a passionate supporter of Greek Independence and fought against the failing Ottoman Empire between 1821 and 1830. He donated much of his considerable fortune to supplying and equipping Greek troops as well as providing humanitarian aid. He is still regarded as a hero in Greece, with a statue in the centre of Athens depicting Greece crowning Byron, and a "Byron's Day" in April.

The poem is based on an account of the siege of Jerusalem by Sennacherib, King of Assyria, found in the second book of Kings in the Old Testament, in which God declares: *"I will defend this city, to save it, for mine own sake, and for my servant David's sake"* (2 Kings 19:34). Whilst the siege of Jerusalem is historic fact (701 BC), Byron uses the biblical account of the heathen Assyrians being struck down by God to create a stirring, heroic account, celebrating God's covenant with the

Hebrews. The poem was published in the book of *Hebrew Melodies* (1815) which were set to music by Isaac Nathan.

Themes

Although the poem's subject is the power of God to overcome the oppressor and deliver justice, the poem is about the **arrogance of aggressors** more generally and **the need to resist tyranny** in any form. In this, Byron foreshadows his later involvement in the Greek struggle for Independence. The image in the opening line, *"like a wolf on the fold"*, has become infamous in literary and popular culture and is often quoted as an exemplar to convey the speed and aggression of anyone, or anything, that is intent on overpowering opposition. The poem generalises **the effect of conflict on the combatants**, as does *"Charge of the Light Brigade"*, and, like that poem, celebrates an unlikely victory with a tone of heroic triumphalism. It is less concerned with the individual human experience, as explored in Hardy's *"The Man He Slew"* or Owen's *"Exposure"*.

Supernatural power is also present in Wordsworth's *"Extract…"*, where Nature or *"unknown modes of being"* are shown to overpower man.

Form, structure and language

The poem is written in *anapaestic tetrametre* which replicates the thundering of horses' hooves. It is the reverse of the rhythm used by Tennyson in *"The Charge of the Light Brigade"* to mimic the rhythm of a gallop. Whereas Byron uses a *metric foot* of two unstressed syllables followed by a stressed syllable (*anapaest*),

Tennyson uses a *dactyl* – one stressed syllable followed by two unstressed. So, *"The Assyrian…"* versus **"Half a league…"** Like Blake, Byron also writes in *rhyming couplets* but the effect, coming at the end of the longer line, is to add to the sense of urgency at the relentless onslaught of the Assyrian forces and later, the scene of devastation caused by the Angel of Death.

In **stanza one**, Byron likens the approaching Assyrian army to a ravening *"wolf"* descending on a helpless flock of sheep in a field. Their arrogance is shown in the colour of their uniforms: *"purple and gold"* are colours associated with royalty. The *alliteration* of *sheen/spears/stars/sea* draws attention to the countless spears of the approaching army, which rolls towards Jerusalem like the waves of the sea of Galilee, their spears shining like stars reflected in the waters.

By the end of **stanza two**, this vast army has been destroyed. The speed of its destruction is conveyed by the *anaphora* of *"Like the leaves…"*, an image of Spring turning to Autumn overnight; the army, which was flourishing and confident (*leaves/green*) is now blown away like withered autumn leaves.

In this and the succeeding stanzas, the depiction of the *"hosts"* destruction moves from the whole army, to the individual horse and rider, then back out to the *"host"*, which gives the scene a chilling realism. The *"Angel of Death"* in **stanza three** may at first be taken as metaphorical. It descends on the army like a *"blast"* of wind, bringing death as they sleep, manifest in the blank, lifeless eyes and stilled hearts of the men.

In **stanza four**, Byron focuses on the detail of the dead horses. Their *"nostrils"* were once wide to draw in the breath they needed for their gallop; now they are wide in death. The image of waves breaking recurs in the *"foam"* which the dying horses breath out, once hot, now cold in death.

Stanza five describes their dead riders, their once bright armour already rusting from the dew that has fallen overnight. The picture then moves outwards to their silent tents, still bright with their banners. The repeated negation *"unlifted"* and *"unblown"* emphasises the speed of their death and the absence of life; they had no time before they were destroyed.

Stanza six shifts the focus back to Assyria, where those left behind mourn their dead and, in their despair, break the statues of their false gods. The *"Gentiles"* are non-believers in the Hebrew God; they have been struck down with merely a *"glance"* from the true God, showing his supernatural speed and strength. Their might melts away like snow in sunlight. The Angel of Death is now made literal.

Extract from "*The Prelude*" – William Wordsworth

Context

Described by Wordsworth as "*the poem on the growth of my own mind*", "*The Prelude*" was intended to precede "*The Recluse*", which he never finished. Essentially, it charts, over 14 books, the influence of Nature and the French Revolution on his sensibilities as a poet. The extract selected here, taken from *Book 1 - Boyhood* could be described as one of the "*spots in time*" that Wordsworth identified as formative moments in his understanding of himself and the world around him:

There are in our existence spots of time,
That with distinct pre-eminence retain
A renovating virtue,   Prelude
Book XII

The Romantics took themselves seriously as men who, through their poetry, could help others understand the world around them. The creative process and the workings of the imagination were worth exploration in themselves, giving us an insight into our relationship to our place in the physical world around us (loosely defined as "Nature") and how we might tap into powers beyond the merely physical. In another age, this could be equated with "religion", but the Romantics were, primarily, atheists and did not equate this awareness of spirituality with any established religion.

Themes

The poem reflects on **the power of nature and the insignificance of man**, of the **imagination** and of **memory**. Sometimes referred to as *"The Stolen Boat"*, the extract describes the young Wordsworth's night-time escapade in a boat. He sets out to row across Ullswater Lake in the Lake District, where he lived for much of his life. Fixing his eyes on the top of a hill to keep his line straight as he rows, as he gets further and further away from land, a much taller peak slowly emerges from behind it. This causes him to be filled with a kind of guilty dread, so he heads back home. The older poet uses this *"spot in time"* to reflect on the power of *"**unknown modes of being**"* – things which we cannot know through our five senses and which we strive to understand spiritually or imaginatively. The crag rising in front of him is both physically powerful and stirs imaginings which bring with them feelings of guilt, dread and helplessness in the face of an unknown real or imagined power. The power of the supernatural or unknown is also shown in Byron's *"The Destruction…"*, but identified with God.

The **power of nature** and apparent **opposition to insignificant Man** is also seen in Owen's *"Exposure"*, where the weather becomes the real enemy of the soldiers. Both poems are notable for their use of literary techniques. *"Extract…"* can be linked thematically to *"Poppies"*, or *"Catrin"*, which explore **the power of memory** to create conflicting feelings within the narrators. All these poems are also intensely personal and autobiographical, giving rise to strong feelings and an examination of the life lived.

Form, structure and language

The extract starts as a *narrative*[7] written in *blank verse:* unrhymed lines of *iambic pentametre*. This regular, compact rhythm (the most common metric form in English poetry) can be compared to the long lines of *iambic hexametre*[8] of Owen's *"Exposure"*. Wordsworth's metre is purposeful as he rows across the lake and back; Owen's long lines reflect the weariness of the soldiers and the drawn-out periods of inactivity as they wait for combat. The reader is guided through the poem by Wordsworth by his use of *enjambment* and *caesura*[9], placing stresses on important words and allowing variation in the rhythm and pace. As often in Wordsworth, the narrative of the opening lines (to line 20) gives way to increased *lyricism*[10] and a change of mood or viewpoint (lines 21 – 34) and ends in reflection (line 35 to end).

The extract opens conversationally enough, although *"(led by her)"* tells us about Wordsworth's intense relationship to the natural world, as he *personifies*[11] nature as *"her"*. He unties the boat and gets in,

---

[7] *Narrative* is a story.
[8] A *hexametre* line has six stressed beats.
[9] See the *Note on Metre* at the end for a fuller explanation of *enjambment* and *caesura*.
[10] *Lyrical* poetry tells of deep feelings or thoughts.
[11] *Personification* is attributing human characteristics to non-human things

seemingly without hesitation. Note the positioning of *"Straight"* at the beginning of line 4, varying the *iambic* rhythm (by using a *trochee*) to emphasise the word. Similarly, weight is given to *"**Pushed**"* in line 5, by the use of the *enjambment* from the preceding line, giving these lines a forward momentum to mimic the movement of the boat:

"**Straight** I /un**loosed**/ her **chain**, /and **step**-/ping in **Pushed** from/the **shore**...

He admits to feeling a little guilty about his activity and suggests that nature has something to say about it (*"Mountain-echoes"*). However, he gives himself up to the pleasures of the moment on his boat ride, indicated by the light imagery of *"circles glittering"*, *"melted"*, *"sparkling light"*, the lapping of water replicated in the repeated "l" sounds. ". His positive attitude continues with the description of the night sky, the use of the word *"elfin"* suggesting that this night is enchanted and special.

The dream begins to turn into a nightmare at line 21, when, behind the crag on which he has *"fixed [his] view"*, a higher peak begins to loom up in the darkness. This peak at once appears threatening, as shown by the *epiphora*[12] of *"a **huge** peak, black and **huge**"*. It too is *personified*, this time as a monster which *"upreared its head"*. The leisurely rowing gives way to an almost

---

[12] *Epiphora* is the repetition of a word or phrase at the end of a sentence or clause. It is the opposite of *anaphora,* where the repetition is at the beginning.

frantic attempt to get away from its presence, in the repeated *"struck and struck again"*, but the *"grim shape"* seems to be following him like a malevolent giant. The words here show its intent: *"Towered"*, *"purpose"*, *"measured"*, *"Strode"*. Note the positioning of the words *"Towered"*, following the *enjambment*, and *"Strode"* at the beginning of the lines for emphasis. The only way to "escape" this monster is, paradoxically, to turn around and row back to land, back towards it (line 29). Now the mood is very different: *"trembling"*, *"silent"*, *"stole"*, *"covert"*[13], *"grave"*, *"serious"*. No time now for watching moonlight rippling on the water!

The *"spectacle"*[14] does not leave him in the days to come. It troubles his thoughts – what might it mean? He has been shown something which he knows to be important, but he does not understand it – it reveals to him *"unknown modes of being"* (line 37). These, for the Romantics, are physical objects in the world (as the black peak clearly is) which also suggest something beyond the merely physical, which could be called "spiritual" or "revelatory"; they tell us about our place in the world and our relationship to it. At the moment, the young Wordsworth has not worked out what this all means, exactly. His mind is a troubled *"blank"* (line 39)– aware that he has seen something important, but unable to process it. Look at how he gropes for words (*"call it"*) to describe how he feels: *"darkness"*,

---

[13] *"covert"* means both a hiding place and a secret.
[14] A *spectacle* is something dramatic that has been seen

"solitude", "desertion". For a poet, his words failing him is bewildering.

His experience affects his whole outlook on the world around him – things are no longer as they once seemed. The surface of the everyday world to which he is accustomed, indicated by the *"trees", "sea", "sky", "fields"*, is overlaid with an awareness of something "other" that exists alongside this, at times hidden (like the peak), at other times revealed to the mind of the poet. What this is, exactly, is left unresolved. Call it *"the power of imagination"*, call it *"Nature"*, *"the meaning of life"*. At this point, Wordsworth is concerned with the recognition of something outside his daily, worldly experience, the meaning of which he will grapple as he grows to maturity as a man and a poet.

Similar feelings of helplessness in the face of an unknown, and potentially hostile power, are found in Owen's *"Exposure"*, where the weather is *personified* as an unseen enemy intent on killing the waiting soldiers.

The Man he Killed – Thomas Hardy

Context

Thomas Hardy was a major novelist of the 19th century as well as a poet. He based many of his stories in the countryside of southwest England, and parts of Dorset, Somerset, Devon and Wiltshire (ancient Wessex) have become known as "Hardy Country". Hardy writes about rural life, unlike Blake whose settings are usually urban. In some ways he is nostalgic, looking back at a mythical "golden age" of country life which was eclipsed by the urbanisation following the Industrial Revolution. He was concerned about the plight of the rural poor and the gap between the working class and the ruling gentry who owned the land on which they worked, a theme seen in Rossetti's *"Cousin Kate"*.

In the latter part of the 19th century, there were a number of wars in which Britain fought to protect its Empire, including the Crimean (1853-1856) and the First and Second Boer Wars (1880-81 and 1899-1902). Hardy, who was opposed to war, wrote this poem in 1902, possibly with reference to the Second Boer War, and it is generally assumed that the *persona* is a soldier who has returned home from this conflict. The title explains that the speaker is reflecting on the experience of killing a man in the war.

Themes

Just as Blake explored the **corrosive power** of anger in *"The Poison Tree"*, so Hardy explores how man can turn against man under the influence of military orders. The soldier also fails to find an answer as to why they are fighting, like the soldiers in *"Exposure"*, shown by the hesitant repetition: *"I shot him dead because – Because he was my foe"*. More broadly, the poem can be seen, like *"Exposure"*, as a comment on **the futility of war**.

Form, structure and language

The poem is written in four-line stanzas, or *quatrains*, with two lines of *iambic trimetre*, followed by one line of *iambic tetrametre* and a final line of *iambic trimetre* (3343). This pattern has similarities with *common* or *ballad* metre, frequently used for folk songs or nursery rhymes. The rhyme scheme is similarly regular, rhyming *abab* throughout. As in Blake's poem, this jaunty rhythm and rhyme is contrasted with the seriousness of the subject matter. It also reflects the rural, and uneducated, origins of the speaker, being a familiar and simpler form than the more sophisticated five-beat (*pentametre*) line of formal verse. The same metre is used by Rossetti in *"Cousin Kate"*, which has a similarly rural setting.

Like *"Cousin Kate"*, the poem is a *dramatic monologue*; Hardy adopts the *persona* of a man from his native Dorset who has returned from a war and reflects on his killing of a young enemy soldier. Hardy uses the *dialect* of southern England to characterise the man's speech. This can be seen in the phrase *"Right many a nipperkin"*, which uses non-standard grammar, and the *dialect* word *"nipperkin"*, meaning a small glass of drink. An early version of the poem made the location of the inn in Dorset. *Dialect* or *patois*[15] is also used to characterise the speaker by Agard in *"Half caste"*, Casey in *"The Class Game"* and Zephaniah in *"No Problem"*, as well as Rossetti in *"Cousin Kate"* to support the theme of **conflict created by socially constructed barriers.**

In **stanza one**, the *persona* reflects on how things might have been, had he met *"the man he killed"* under different circumstances. They would have enjoyed similar, simple pleasures, such as having a pint together at a local pub, acknowledging their common humanity, undivided by country or politics.

Stanza two continues his reflection, explaining the difference between meeting someone in normal life and coming "face to face" with someone whom, you have been told, as a soldier, is your enemy. Clearly, his opponent has been told the same (*"as he at me"*); it is a question of who fires first.

In **stanza three**, the man tries to explain why he shot him, but his explanation is unconvincing, even to himself. His hesitation is conveyed by the hyphen and repetition of *"because – Because"*; the attempt to reassure himself that the man was an enemy with the *"Just so:"*; the unconvincing *"of course he was"*. Hardy also breaks the regular rhythm with the *caesura* [16]after *"Just so:"* and *"clear enough"* to add to the impression

---

[15] Agard was born in British Guyana, whilst Zephaniah was born and grew up in Birmingham amongst a Jamaican community. They use a very similar *patois*.

[16] A *caesura* is a break in the middle of a metric line

of doubt. The last word "*although*" introduces a second thought – maybe there is another explanation for the man being there? Hardy uses *enjambment* to carry this idea into the next stanza.

Stanza four gives an alternative view of the "*foe*". He is a man like the speaker who enlisted because he was down on his luck and could think of nothing better to do. Unemployed, having sold his only asset, the traps with which he could catch (or poach) game, he decided to join up to get a wage, food and a place to live. He had no intention of killing his fellow man. Going to war was unconnected with the reality. Hardy uses *dialect* here to emphasise the casual simplicity of the men's thinking, and their innocence.

In **stanza five**, the man exclaims on the idiocy of his situation and of war; the words "*quaint*" and "*curious*", both meaning odd or peculiar, being an understatement, or *litotes,* to emphasise the ridiculousness of his situation. Had he met his "*foe*" in a pub, he would have bought him a drink or lent him some money.

The poem leaves the reader with a feeling of unease as the speaker seems rather casual about his responsibility for killing a man. However, the conversational, casual tone, created by the rhythm and use of *dialect*, masks Hardy's anger as he shows how natural fellow-feeling between people is corrupted by a political or social agenda.

Cousin Kate – Christian Rossetti

Context

Critics of Christina Rossetti refer to her "ambiguity", her teasing, questioning voice which challenges the readers' interpretation of her poems and the apparent conflicts in her approach to themes of spirituality and sexuality. Rossetti's perspective is often from someone dead or contemplating her death. Much is infused with a sense of the loss of love, or the opportunity for love, although whether this is love in a religious or secular context is not always clear. Love and death seem at times inextricably linked. She never married, although she received proposals three times. She suffered from life-long fragile health, dying from Grave's Disease, a disorder of the thyroid gland, in 1894, aged 64.

As in Hardy's poem, *"Cousin Kate"* is set in rural England and, like the man in Hardy's poem, the speaker is of a lower class, which is the key to the drama which unfolds. The class system in England during the 19th century was rigid; there were few opportunities to move up the social ladder, particularly for a woman, save by marriage. There were also strict social taboos on sex outside of marriage. The seduction of an innocent country girl by a man from a higher class was a common subject in Victorian fiction, including *"Tess of the D'Urbervilles"* by Thomas Hardy. Children born "out of wedlock", and their mothers, were shunned by society, and dependent on relatives for support. Some children were passed off as the sons and daughters of their grandmother. Many were abandoned and brought up in orphanages under harsh regimes and sold into virtual slavery. The experiences of one such orphan was novelised by Charles Dickens in *"Oliver Twist"*.

Themes

Rossetti, like Hardy, Zephaniah and Agard, are asking questions about **how society is organised**, the nature of **social and economic power** and the **social constructs** that divide us.

"Cousin Kate" is a social drama in miniature showing the **conflict between family members** (although *"Cousin"* could mean a close friend) and the **conflict between social classes** in a rigidly divided society, as well as the relative powerlessness of women. In this Rossetti expresses similar ideas to Agard in *"Half caste"*, Casey in *"The Class Game"* and Zephaniah in *"No Problem"*. Like Hardy in *"The Man He Killed"*, Rossetti sees such barriers as artificial, **social constructs which deny our common humanity and create unnecessary pain and suffering.** Rossetti and Hardy both show that the antagonists – the *"killed man"* and *"Cousin Kate"* - have much in common with the speaker; they are the same, but in different circumstances.

Form, structure and language

Rossetti also uses a form of *ballad metre* for this *dramatic monologue* set in rural England; lines of four (*tetrametre*) and three beat lines (*trimetre*) with a regular rhyme scheme *ababcbcb*. Despite this regularity, Rossetti captures the rhythms of speech, and the emotions of the speaker, by varying the pattern of *metric feet,* rather than maintaining a more rigid pattern like Hardy. For example, in lines 19-20, the *iambic* pattern (*light/**heavy**-*) of "He **saw** you **at** your **fa**ther's **gate**" is followed by a s*pondee* – two heavy beats – on "***Chose you***" to show her anger at her former lover, as she seems to point the finger at Cousin Kate.

Rossetti uses repetition, particularly of questions, a common feature of ballads, as in: *"Why did a great lord…?"* which adds to the *pathos* of the speaker's situation as she searches for a sense of justice in this harsh world.

The poem is a *dramatic monologue*, the speaker being a young, innocent country girl ("*cottage-maiden*") who has been seduced and abandoned by a local Lord in favour of her "*Cousin Kate*". The speaker rails against her fate, primarily addressing her anger towards "Kate", whom the speaker sees as being undeserving of the good fortune she has won. She went with the Lord out of love – Kate holds him off until she gets a promise of marriage. However, the speaker has the final triumph. She has a son by the Lord, which Kate does not, and she knows this is something the Lord wants above all else.

In **stanza one**, the back-story is given. The speaker, who is a contented and innocent "*cottage-maid*", is noticed by a local member of the ruling classes, a "great lord", who flatters her, praising her prettiness and blonde (*flaxen*) hair. She asks rhetorically why this should have happened to her, the repeated questions showing her pain at her present circumstances.

In **stanza two,** we learn that the girl was seduced into going with the Lord, attracted by the beautiful house he lived in, to become his mistress. The word *"plaything"* suggests that he was not serious about this relationship, but using the girl for his pleasure, only to discard her when he becomes bored. At first, she is like a precious, ornamental jewel to him, a *"golden knot"* which he wears with pride, but *"knot"* also suggests she is tied to him – until he loosens it. Later, she is discarded, changed for a different woman, *"like a glove"* that has become unfashionable. As a result, she is shamed (being no longer a virgin and so, *"unclean"*), when, had she been left alone, she would have remained pure and at peace with her life.

Stanza three is addressed to Cousin Kate, now *"Lady Kate"*, as she has married the Lord, after he exchanges the *"cottage-maid"* for his new love. The Lord has been watching Kate as she goes about her daily life in the village, just as he watched his former love, and decides to make her his new one.

Stanza four suggests that Kate remained a virgin (*"good and pure"*) until she became the Lord's wife, unlike the speaker; he could only "bind" Kate to him by marrying her. The *"golden ring"* is contrasted with the *"golden knot"*. The repetition of *"good and pure"* is ironic – she sees Kate as neither, but as calculating. But Kate's calculation, rather than the speaker's true feelings of love, have paid off. The speaker is now an "outcast" shunned by the villagers as a "fallen woman". The force of her emotions is evident in the image of her cast down in the "dust" and "howling", like a wounded animal, in despair. In contrast, Kate sits carefree in golden splendour, like a pet bird in a golden cage. The imagery of birds links back to the *"dove"* of stanza two, an image of the gentle creature the speaker was before she was seduced, and forward to *"stronger wing"* – Kate's ambition.

She asks which of the two of them showed more love towards their Lord? She cannot answer but acknowledges that Kate was more resolute in getting what she wanted. *"Stronger wing"* suggests that Kate was ambitious in flying higher, holding out until she got what she wanted.

This comment on the bargaining power of virginity is a bold statement for Rossetti to make in her time. She was part of the Pre-Raphaelite Brotherhood (her brother was Dante Gabriel Rossetti, the painter) who were notoriously liberal in their approach to sexuality and lived in an easy-going community of artists and writers where relationships were fluid. Here, Rossetti is commenting on Victorian sexual hypocrisy.

Stanza five confirms that the speaker believes Kate's love to be false *("writ in sand"* and therefore temporary) whereas hers was true. She asserts that if their roles had been reversed and the Lord had picked out Kate first, rather than her, then Kate would have rejected the Lord's advances as she did not love him, spitting in his face. She only went with the Lord to raise her status by becoming his wife.

Stanza six shows the speaker has her revenge on Cousin Kate. She reveals that she has a son, and that Kate has not, nor seems likely to have one, despite all her material wealth, and it threatens her. The final *quatrain* is addressed to the speaker's son, drawing him close. He is both her *"shame"*, as he and she are despised by society with its rigid codes, but also her *"pride"* as he came from love. Having a son, for men in positions of power and wealth, was important, as only a son could inherit their lands and titles. The son must be born in wedlock – he cannot be illegitimate. She knows that her Lord would have given anything to have a son and heir, but by giving up the speaker, he has given up his hope for the future of his name.

The poem is full of bitterness and anger; an awful realisation that in following her heart rather than her head, the speaker has ruined her life and placed a heavy burden on her illegitimate son. Although written in the regular, sing-song rhythm of ballad metre, the effect created using emphasis and repetition is very different from Hardy's speaker's bewildered musing on the death of a stranger.

Half-caste – John Agard

Context

Agard was born in former British Guiana, in the Caribbean, but moved to England as a young man in the 1970s. He has become a popular performance poet and is regularly on the GCSE syllabus. He is married to fellow Guyanian poet Grace Nichols. His poetry often comments on the social status of immigrants from the Caribbean and he writes in a version of the local *patois*. The poem is included in the collection *"Half-caste"* (2005) which explores the experience of immigrants from the Caribbean living in England.

"Half-caste" generally means a person who is born to parents of different ethnicities, as was Agard. It is a term that is now considered racist and has been largely abandoned in favour of the more neutral "mixed race", but it was in common use at the time Agard came to England. The term has associations with racial purity, being derived from the word *"casta"*, or pure, in Spanish. It is also used to denote the *caste* system in India, by which people are segregated into strict social hierarchies.

Themes

In this highly personal poem, Agard rails at the denigration of people of mixed race, showing the absurdity of categorising or stereotyping them, and discriminating against them, as if they were made up of two distinctly different halves. He does this by giving examples in art and nature of how differences combine to make a new, and wonderful, whole, worthy of celebration.

In common with *"The Man He Killed"*, *"Cousin Kate"*, *"The Class Game"* and *"No Problem"*, Agard explores the **social constructs which deny our common humanity and create conflict, leading to unnecessary pain and suffering**. Agard, like the other poets, shows how such stereotyping dehumanises people, and is both hurtful and absurd. However, unlike Hardy and Rossetti who use the *dramatic monologue*, Agard presents his personal perspective and his own experience, as does Casey in *"The Class Game"* and Zephaniah in *"No Problem"*.

Form, language and structure

The *monologue* is written in *free verse*[17], but with predominantly two and three beat lines, which, together with the frequent repetition, give it a strong rhythmic pulse, as if chanted or rapped. Indeed, Agard frequently performs this piece at conventions. The opening imperatives *"Excuse me"* and the repeated *"Explain yuself"* sets the tone of indignation as Agard challenges the listener's preconceptions of people of mixed ethnicity.

Apart from the opening and closing *triads* (three lines), the poem is written in one long, stanza with minimal punctuation. This suggests that Agard is ranting angrily

---

[17] *Free verse* is poetry that neither rhymes nor has a regular rhythm (or *metre*)

at his listener. However, Agard uses the repeated *"Explain yuself/wha yu mean/when yu say half-caste",* as a chorus (together with the occasional "/" denoting the end of a question) to break the poem into distinct sections, as he explores the absurdity of the concept of *"half-caste".*

The poem is written in a form of Caribbean *dialect* or *patois.* Agard reproduces the speakers accent with his unconventional spelling and non-standard grammar, rather than using a distinct vocabulary. The use of this *dialect* brings authenticity to the words and ideas of the speaker, as in Hardy's *"The Man He Killed"* or Zephaniah's *"No Problem"* or Casey's *"The Class Game".*

In the **opening *triad,*** Agard sets out his position as a *"half-caste"* man. The interjection *"Excuse me"* suggests that he has overheard someone using the term *"half-caste"*, which he feels compelled to challenge. *"standing on one leg"* is the first of a number of absurdities he uses to mock his imagined listener.

The first section beginning *"Explain yuself/wha you mean"* continues this scenario, asking the listener what he means by the term *"half-caste".* He gives an example from Art to show the nonsense of splitting something whole into its constituent parts. Picasso was a 20th century cubist painter, one of whose most famous paintings, *"Weeping Woman"* (1937), is composed of red and green geometric shapes.

The next section (following the "/") takes an example from nature, the mix of *"light an shadow"* in the sky which together make up a weather pattern. If you call that "half-caste", he suggests, then you might as well say that English weather is always "half-caste", referring to the belief that it is always rainy. In fact, he jokes, it is not so much *"half-caste"* as *"overcast"*, making a pun on the word "cast", which means "covered" with clouds, which deliberately block out the sun. *"ah (I) rass"* in Caribbean slang is a swearword, showing anger. Again, the "/" shows the end of this example.

The next section uses an example from music. Tchaikovsky was a 19th century Russian composer of symphonies, ballets and concerti. Agard imagines him composing his symphonies (which are orchestral pieces) on the piano, which has white and black keys, mixing the notes together to create his music. Agard points out the futility of attempting to separate the music into the individual black and white notes.

A longer section follows in which he turns to himself as an example. He challenges the listener with the nonsense of splitting himself into two halves, so that he listens with one ear, sees with one eye and shakes hands with half a hand. He sleeps at night with half an eye shut, casting only half a shadow in the moonlight. The repeated "*I*" at the beginning of alternate lines and repeated "half" here adds urgency which suggests exasperation at the use of the term *"half-caste"*.

The final admonition to his listener is to return the next day and give him his "whole" attention (the listener presumably being white, British and therefore "undivided") so that he can tell him his full story.

Exposure – Wilfred Owen

Context

A popular contemporary saying about World War 1 was *"We went to war with Rupert Brooke and came home with Siegfried Sassoon"*, a comment on the length of the war itself (1914-18), the number of poets that flourished during the period and the changing attitudes to the War that their poetry expresses. In temperament, the early War poets were more aligned to Tennyson than to Owen or Sassoon; Rupert Brooke's *"The Soldier"* sees dying for one's country as a patriotic adventure:

"That there's some corner of a foreign field
That is forever England".

As the war that was supposed to be *"over by Christmas"* dragged into its third year, attitudes at home and in the trenches changed, with public criticism of the decisions being taken by the Military and the heavy loss of life. Most of Owen's poetry was written from 1917 to 1918 and published posthumously. He was encouraged to write by the poet Siegfried Sassoon, whom he met whilst convalescing at Craiglockhart Hospital following a diagnosis of shell shock. Having returned to the front-line, he was killed a week before the Armistice, which ended the war in November 1918.

Themes

In the preface to his proposed first collection of poetry, Owen wrote:

This book is not about heroes. English poetry is not yet fit to speak of them.
Nor is it about deeds, or lands, nor anything about glory, honour, might, majesty, dominion, or power, except War.
Above all I am not concerned with Poetry.
My subject is War, and the pity of War.
The Poetry is in the pity.

The title, *"Exposure"*, refers to: the men's exposure to the elements, which form a major part of the description of the hardships they face; the effect of that exposure, which is death; Owen's own purpose in writing – to expose, or show, the horrors of the War to the public back at home.

Wilfred Owen was a soldier on the front-line, as were many of the poets, and documented the appalling conditions in the trenches, and **the effect of conflict on the individual soldier**, whilst asking the question "What is this all for?" The question is shared by Tennyson (*"The whole world wonder'd"*) and by Hardy in "The Man He Killed". In Owen's documentation of the individual human experience, his poem is close to the interpretation of the effects of war in *"War Photographer"* and *"Belfast Confetti"*.

Owen's poems often suggest that the whole world is "out of joint" because of the War; **Nature itself has become hostile** and unpredictable and is oblivious to human suffering, whilst God is absent entirely. This **enmity between Man and Nature** has echoes in Wordsworth's *"The Prelude"*.

Form, Structure and Language

The poem is a monologue written predominantly in *hexametres,* lines with six stressed beats, with some variation in the metrical pattern. These long, faltering lines can be compared with the urgent galloping of horses in the regular *dimetre* of Tennyson's poem, or Byron's *tetrametres* and rhyming couplets, or Wordsworth regular *iambic* lines. Owen's men are held in a nightmare where *"nothing happens"*, reflected in these long lines that seem to go on forever. There is a regular rhyming pattern of *abba,* but instead of full rhymes, Owen uses *pararhyme*, changing the vowels whilst retaining a similar pattern of consonants in the final words on the line, again suggesting that the world is no longer held together by any rational thought: *knive us/nervous*; *silent/salient*; *wire/war*; *brambles/rumbles*. There is a recurring structural feature in the short *refrain* with which each stanza ends, which asks and answers Owen's questions about the purpose of this War, in an endless cycle:

But nothing happens
What are we doing here?
Is it that we are dying?
We turn back to our dying
For love of God seems dying
But nothing happens.

The constant questioning is reminiscent of Levertov's approach to seeking answers in *"What Were They Like?"*, to Zephaniah's in *"No Problem"* and Agard's in *"Half-caste"*. It is the questioning of people caught up in a conflict not of their own making which nevertheless disrupts their lives forever.

Throughout, Owen uses extensive *alliteration, sibilance* and *assonance* to evoke the sights and sounds around him, as well as *metaphor* and *simile*. In this, the poem can be compared to Wordsworth's *"Extract..."* which is similarly rich in literary techniques. The poem is also notable for the use of *pathetic fallacy*[18].

The **first stanza** sets the tone of the whole: a nightmare world in which Owen uses *pathetic fallacy* to show how the men's misery is matched by the merciless weather. The cold takes on substance and attacks (*"knives"*) the men, both physically and mentally, as they await the next stage in the battle – which fails to come. Long periods of inactivity followed by brief and bloody engagements were a familiar pattern of warfare in the trenches. The men, although tired, cannot sleep, as the silence brings a mounting tension about what might be about to happen, as signified by the whispering lookouts, their anxiety conveyed by the *sibilance* and *asyndetic listing*: *"whisper, curious, nervous."*

In the **second stanza**, Owen deepens the nightmare by using a *simile*, likening the wind buffeting the entanglements of barbed wire to the movements caused by men caught up in it while crossing no-man's-

---

[18]*Pathetic fallacy* (literally *"false feeling"*) describes weather or landscape as if it is in sympathy with the human subject of the poem. For example, wet and cold when he is miserable, sunny when happy.

land. The distortion of nature is emphasised by the *metaphor* for the wire as *"brambles"*. The men seem detached from the real world; the sound of guns *"Far off"* seems to have no relevance to their situation, isolated in the cold silence around them.

In **stanza three**, dawn-break beings no respite; instead, it begins to rain heavily. The *"melancholy army"* is a metaphor for the banks of storm clouds that move in from the east, again depicting Nature, as well as man, being at war with the men shivering below. Owen uses *hypallage* here, or a *transferred epithet*; it is the men *"shivering"* rather than the clouds that bring the cold rain, but the transfer from one to the other binds the two together in this misery.

Stanza 4 opens with a flurry of activity, the whistle of streaking bullets conveyed by the *sibilant* "s" in *"**S**udden /**s**uccessive /flight**s** /bullet**s**/**s**treak /**s**ilence"*. But it is a false alarm. The bullets do no more, or less, than the snow which has begun to fall around them. Again, notice the use of *hypallage* with *"shudders"*, transferred to the snow-filled air from the shivering men below. The snowflakes (note the alliterated *"flowing/flakes/flocks"* to suggest softly falling snow) swirl around aimlessly like great *"flocks"* of birds. Owen may well be thinking of the evening flights of starlings (called a *"murmur"*) that create intricate patterns in the sky as they flock in their thousands, moving together, pausing and changing direction, the reasons for which we cannot understand. The wind is *"nonchalant"* (casual), without purpose, like the waiting men.

As the snow deepens **in stanza 5,** the men begin to suffer from the effects of *exposure* – they feel drowsy and the snow begins to feel warm as their body temperature drops. The snow is *personified* as the icy fingers of Death. They begin to hallucinate – are they now feeling the spring sun, surrounded by the blossoms falling from trees, disturbed by a feeding blackbird hunting for insects, as it did at home in England? Their vision of home, and their growing lassitude[19], is beautifully and intensely realised in the repeated "*l*" sounds: "*Littered/blossoms/trickling/blackbird*". Unable to rouse themselves, they wonder, helplessly, if they are dying.

In **stanza 6,** the realisation of impending death "drags" them further home to deserted houses where once they lived. They are near-abandoned – the fires have been allowed to sink to embers ("*glozed*" is a form of "glossed", as in a thin shining covering of fire) and crickets and mice have taken over. They cannot go back – they are fast becoming ghosts in reality, and they have already become ghosts to those left behind. This is another recurring Owen theme – that, if not forgotten, the men sent to the front quickly became "ghosts" to wives and sweethearts, as if already dead.

---

[19] *Lassitude* means lack of energy or purpose

There is a terrible poignancy and helplessness in the *epiphora*[20] at the end of *"all closed; on us the doors are closed"*. All that is left to them is to endure and die.

Stanza seven reflects on the men's feelings about the cause for which they are dying. They believe that only by dying can those at home be saved; *"kind fires"* is *metonomy*[21], using a feature of something to indicate the thing itself. So, *"kind fires"* is a substitute expression for the home and those who live within it. Only through the soldiers' deaths can those at home live happily under a *"true"* sun – a way of life that opposes the oppressor (the Germans) whose political aims precipitated the war. The soldiers are afraid that God will not come to save their loved ones and their way of life – they are *"made afraid"* in their love. So, they are willing (*"not loath"*) to endure the suffering in the trenches; it makes them *"born"* again, even if their faith in God, and God's love for them, seems to be *"dying"*.

This is a radical statement for Owen to make. Although belief in a God was already on the wane before the War, there is little doubt that after it, Britain's move towards a more secular society was accelerated. Between the Crimean War and the Great War, methods of communication advanced significantly and news,

---

[20] *Epiphora* means repetition at the end of a sentence or clause; it is the opposite of *anaphora*, which means repetition at the beginning of a clause: *"half a league, half a league"*
[21] *Metonomy* can also be illustrated by the term *"Golden Arches"* for *"MacDonald's"*.

together with postcards and letters from soldiers, were brought back from the Front in a matter of hours or days, together with photographs of the widespread destruction caused by the heavy shelling of towns and villages in Flanders and the Somme. Support for the war waned throughout 1917-18 as the death toll rose higher. In the face of such loss of life, many people's belief in a benevolent God was severely tested.

The **final stanza** returns to the harsh realities of the men's situation and the prospect of death from freezing arriving in the night. Owen shifts the tense from the present to the future, imagining the patrols that will go out in the morning to bury the dead with their *"picks and shovels"*. Notice the positioning of *"Pause"* at the beginning of line 38 to give it emphasis and create a "pause". The images of the dead men are deliberately graphic: *"shrivelling/ puckering/crisp/eyes are ice"* as he unflinchingly recalls the frozen dead men that he himself has seen. The final image of the *"eyes as ice"* suggests that their eyes were open as they watched their death approach, the clear liquid in the eyes freezing.

The poem ends with the refrain *"But nothing happens"*. There has been no engagement – they are still waiting; nothing happens as the patrols go out – the men are dead and beyond help; there are no consequences from their death – nothing happens to end the war and it drags on, futilely.

The Charge of the Light Brigade - Alfred, Lord Tennyson

Context

Alfred Tennyson, 1st Baron Tennyson, was a favourite of Queen Victoria and poet laureate from 1850 until his death in 1892. Poet Laureate is a public appointment, in the gift of the monarch, which requires the holder to write poetry for certain state and national occasions. *"The Charge of the Light Brigade"* was written within six weeks of the Battle of Balaclava in 1854, an engagement in the Crimean War (1853-1856), during which the charge took place, and was published in the national newspaper *"The Enquirer"*. The charge is infamous for the loss of life, caused by transmitting confused orders. The Light Brigade, a lightly-armed and armoured cavalry unit of around 670 men, led by Lord Cardigan, instead of being sent to harass retreating Russians and stop them moving guns, was sent into an enclosed valley to storm a gun placement manned by the opposing Russian troops, which was heavily defended on all sides. More than 150 men were killed, another 122 wounded and 350 horses died or were destroyed afterwards. The poem praises the heroism of the cavalrymen whilst acknowledging, but not exploring, the "bungling" that led to the charge being ordered. The action prompted the French Marshall, Pierre Bosquet, to pronounce: *"C'est magnifique, mais ce n'est pas la guerre. C'est de la folie"*. (*"It is magnificent, but it is not war. It is madness."*)

The Crimean War was one of the earliest to be regularly reported by newspaper reporters and cameramen "in the field". News of events at the front reached Britain only three weeks later and it was the eye-witness account of William Howard Russell, reporting for the *Times,* that formed the basis for Tennyson's poem. This explains the comment that *"All the world wonder'd"*, as news of the engagement reached the public in an unprecedentedly short time. The circumstances surrounding the Charge were the subject of controversy in the newspapers, and in parliament, with accusations made on all sides as to who was responsible for the *"blunder"*, in which the lightly armoured Light Brigade (instead of the better equipped Heavy Brigade) were sent up against a fixed nest of Russian guns positioned at the head of a valley, protected on two sides by gun emplacements on the surrounding hills.

Themes

As poet laureate, it is perhaps unsurprising that Tennyson should write this poem as a *eulogy*[22] – a poem praising **heroism in conflict,** rather than openly criticising the decisions of those in charge. It is not entirely uncritical, however, of the decisions taken that led to the charge. There is a clear distinction made throughout, between those who gave the orders and those who carried them out, with the focus on the latter. In the original version, the supposed source of the *"blunder"* was named as "Nolan", who carried the

---

[22]An *eulogy* is a poem of praise. Do not confuse with *elegy*, which is a poem for the dead.

orders, but this was later anonymised by Tennyson to refocus on the men. There is also an ambiguity in the word *"wonder'd"*, which can indicate both awe and questioning.

Although the circumstances of the charge are documented in some detail and the horror acknowledged, Tennyson's poem approaches the Light Brigade as a single, indivisible unit of war, with little focus on individual suffering. A similar approach can be seen in Byron's *"The Destruction…"*. In this, it can be contrasted with the cold realities depicted by Owen in *"Exposure"*, or the cynicism of *"War Photographer"*, or the confusion of *"Belfast Confetti"*, which take a closer look at **the effects of conflict on the individual.** Perhaps this reflects a more modern attitude to war, starting with Owen during the First World War and continuing ever since, with the rise of a more individualistic culture, less bound by conventions laid down by the State and Religion than in Tennyson's time, and the increasing power of the media to report on events in real time. **The role of the media in reporting Conflict**, is reflected in both *"Belfast Confetti"*, *"War Photographer"* and *"What Were They Like?"*.

Form, structure and language

Tennyson's *narrative poem* is unique in its persistent use of rhythm, rhyme and *anaphora* to convey the mad charge of the light cavalry into the *"Valley of Death"*. It is written in a regular *dactylic dimetre* – two stressed beats in each line, with each metric *foot* being a *dactyl* – **Tum**-*ti-ti*,[23] to represent the thunderous charge of the horses galloping. It can be likened to Byron's use of an *anapaestic* line, also chosen to represent hoofbeats. The frequent *repetition* and use of *full rhyme*[24] give further emphasis, propelling the verse forwards, whilst keeping it under tight control. Note that this *repetition* occurs at the end of lines as well as the beginning, giving frequent repetitions of rhymes. The middle lines of each stanza also rhyme with each other: *"hundred", "blunder'd", "thunder'd", wonder'd", "thunder'd", "wonder'd"*, underpinning the dichotomy between the heroism of the action and the folly of it.

Each of the six sections of the poem are arranged as a single stanza – Tennyson simply adds to or reduces the number of lines in the stanza to accommodate the story he wants to tell. Section 1 describes the giving of the orders to charge; section 2 gives the men's unquestioning response to them; section 3 describes the charge into the Valley; section 4 describes the engagement with the enemy; section 5 shows the retreat up the Valley; section 6 praises the men's heroism, addressing his national audience.

Section 1 establishes the circumstances for the charge, using the reported orders that created the confusion, although leaving the *"He"* unidentified. Tennyson originally attributed them to Captain Nolan who carried the orders, which originated from Lord Raglan, to Lord Lucan, who commanded the Cavalry. It was the identity

---

[23] See the section on *Metre* at the end of this guide.
[24] Full rhyme is where the whole word rhymes with another, as in *"thunder'd/wonder'd"*

of *"the guns"* that caused the confusion. The *"Valley of Death"* is a reference to Psalm 23: *"Even though I walk through the valley of the shadow of death, I will fear no evil"*. Here Tennyson substitutes the metaphoric *"valley"* for a real one.

Section 2 imagines the Unit's response – although aware of the "blunder", they accept their orders unquestioningly. This may be Tennyson writing with the benefit of hindsight; it is not clear that Lord Cardigan, who led the charge and survived, realised the error until after the event. However, it raises the patriotic tone and again places emphasis on the men rather than their leaders. Notice the use of the *anaphora* with *"Theirs"* placed forcefully at the beginning of lines 13 – 15 and mirrored by the regular full rhymes on *"reply"*, *"why"* and *"die"* at the end of each *end-stopped*[25] line.

Section 3 describes the positioning of the guns in the valley – lined up along the valley walls, so that the men become easy targets as they ride between them. Tennyson uses the *anaphora* of *"Cannons"* at the start of the lines together with the *epiphora* of *"of them"* to mimic the narrowness of the canyon they are riding down and the overwhelming firepower that confronts them. There is a rare use of *enjambment* at *"volley'd and thunder'd"* to focus attention on the sound imagery. He repeats the reference to the Psalm and

---

[25] *End-stopped* means that the meaning of the line is complete at the end of it; it is the opposite of *enjambment*, where the sense is carried over to the next line.

also introduces the image of Hell as a wide-open mouth, common in Anglo-Saxon and medieval *iconography*[26].

In **section 4,** the Light Brigade engage with the enemy, brandishing their swords which *"flash"* in the sun, the word suggesting both speed and ferocity. The juxtaposition of *"Sabring"* and *"gunners"* underlines the imbalance between the two forces, as does the word *"army"*, with the Light Cavalry outnumbered and "outgunned". *"All the world wonder'd"* is a comment on the remarks of the Commanders of the allied forces on the action during the events, but also shows that warfare at this time was moving into the modern age of reporters and cameramen – both of whom covered the war (see "**context**"). The scene is brought vividly to life in the use of verbs of violent action: *"Charging"*, *", Plunged", Reel'd"*, all opening the lines, and the alliterated *"Shatter'd and sunder'd"*. Their action was swift, ferocious and deadly. However, they do not come out unscathed. Triumph gives way to bitter realisation in the repetition of *"Then they rode back, but **not/Not** the six hundred."*

Section 5 tracks the unit's return up the valley, the cannons still raining death and destruction upon them. The stanza is almost a repetition of section 3, altered to show the terrible toll of death. *"Boldly they rode and well"* gives way to the alliterated *"While horse and hero fell."* But some escape the *"jaws of Death"* – *"all that*

---

[26] *Iconography* means pictures or symbols

was left of them" – which is, of course, a miracle, in religious symbolism.

Section 6 gives way to Tennyson's praise of the Light Brigade with a *rhetorical question* addressed to the public reader and the repetition of the opinion that this was an event that was of world-importance, not just an act of heroism and gallantry of importance to the British. Line 53 is an exhortation to the public to *"Honour...!"* these men and their heroic deed.

The poem is often taken as an uncritical response to the Charge, portraying it as an unquestioning salute to heroic sacrifice for Queen and Country. Whilst it celebrates the bravery of the Brigade, however, it is not without an oblique commentary on those who, whether through negligence or simple error, caused it to happen. In this, it can be compared with Hardy's understated anger at the death of *"The Man he Killed"*.

Catrin – Gillian Clarke

Context

Gillian Clarke is a Welsh poet who for some time was the equivalent of the Poet Laureate for Wales. Catrin is Gillian Clarke's daughter. At the time she wrote this poem, Catrin was a young teenager. The poet looks back to her daughter's birth, reflecting on the relationship between a mother and daughter over time, as Catrin stands in front of her mother demanding that she be allowed to *"skate in the dark"* for a little longer.

Themes

The poem explores **the changing relationship between a mother and daughter** over time, which gives rise to a conflict between them. Birth is likened to a *"struggle"* between the two, the baby trying to break free of the mother's womb and the mother trying to release the child, but still tied to her by the umbilical-chord. This "struggle" persists as the child grows up and strives to be independent. This theme is also found in *"Poppies"*, as a mother mourns her child going to school for the first time, but realises, from the way he runs off *"intoxicated"*, that the wider world of adolescence beckons. Both *"Catrin"* and *"Poppies"* are notable for the small details that depict the conflict between mother and child, particularly the focus on the *"hair"* of both children – one, *"straight, strong, long, brown"* showing the child's challenge, the other *"gelled blackthorns"* which defy the mother's touch.

The poem could also be compared to *"Extract from the Prelude"* where the easy, natural relationship between man and nature is challenged by a wider view of the world that rises gradually, but inevitably, between the young man and his familiar surroundings. All three poems look to an uncertain future where the norms of relationships will be challenged.

Form, structure and language

Although at first reading the poem may appear to be in free verse, it is written in loose *trimetres,* (lines with three stresses) and with significant use of near or para-rhymes, as at *"child/white/lights/tight"*, *"circles/ourselves"*, *"struggle/strong, long"* and *"rosy/rope"* which give it an apparently loose, but actually, tight structure, which is in keeping with the theme of invisible ties that bind mothers and daughters together. The poem is given impetus (forward movement) by extensive use of *enjambment* and *caesura,* as in:

*"It was a square
Environmental blank, disinfected
Of paintings or toys."*

This also enables Clarke to create surprise in the juxtaposition of the image of the sterile hospital ward and the signs of new life in the *"paintings or toys"*.

The poem opens with Clarke addressing her daughter (*"child"*), remembering the day of her daughter's birth, as she watched the traffic outside the window of the delivery room in hospital as she prepares to give birth. The opening *direct address* to her daughter, and the positioning of the word *"child"* at the end of the line, suggests that the mother has "defiance" in common with her daughter. The changing traffic lights suggest the change about to happen in her life. The strength of the memory is shown by the *anaphora* (repeated opening words) *"I can remember you..."*. The *"first fierce confrontation"*, is the struggle to be born, emphasised by the alliteration. The *"red rope"* is the umbilical cord which binds the two together, the mother struggling to give birth, the child struggling to break free of the womb - a tug of war between them. The delivery room is clean, bare and clinical – *"an environmental blank"*, which bears no signs of the child who is to come. As she gives birth, the mother cries out and the child cries in answer, the noise filling the room. The verb *"wrote"* is a metaphor, as if these cries were drawings a child has scribbled on the white tiled walls. Both mother and daughter cry out to be free of each other.

The **second stanza** recognises that mother and daughter can never be free of one another. They are bound together by invisible ties. The struggle that happened in that hospital room (the *"glass tank"*) continues down the years. The image of the *"glass tank"* suggests the incubators new-born babies are sometimes placed in. It is *"clouded"* as the feelings of mother and child are confused and fill the room and the future is uncertain. The word *"change"* links back to the changing traffic lights in the first stanza. She realises that the two are still "*fighting*" – struggling for their independence one from another – as her daughter stands defiantly in front of her.

The child is vividly sketched. The *internal rhyme* in the adjectives "*straight, strong, long*" add to the image of strength, the reveal of the noun "hair" delayed by the use of *enjambment* - "*long/brown hair*" - so the softer image does not undermine the initial impression. *Enjambment* is used again with "*rosy/Defiant*", this time in reverse, as the child's soft, pink cheeks are revealed as being the healthy skin of a young girl, but also her heightened emotion as she confronts her mother. The defiance recalls the struggle of her birth, the umbilical cord, although cut, still lying beneath the surface of their relationship. Clarke has said the image of the "*old rope*" is of a boat tied to a harbour wall (a safe haven), hidden below the surface of the water. As the emotion between them heightens, so the link between them tightens, and just as a rope under water rises as it tightens, dripping water, so old emotions surface, the word "*trailing*" showing that feelings cannot be put aside. They bring conflicting emotions, both "*love and conflict*", as the mother acknowledges that her protective love for her daughter (who wants to stay out "*in the dark*") is at odds with her daughter's defiant desire for autonomy. Ending the poem with the child's not unreasonable request to be allowed to skate (roller skates – not ice-skates) for another hour, is a way of showing how powerful the protective motherly instinct is, and perhaps how easy it is to become blinded to her daughter's needs by her own, overpowering emotions.

War Photographer – Carole Satyamurti

Context

Carole Satyamurti is an English poet, lecturer and sociologist. The poem was written in 1987, at a time when there were a number of major conflicts, including the Iran/Iraq war, which this poem seems to reference with the line *"first bomb of the morning"*, suggesting a prolonged campaign in which civilians were targets. War photography is as old as the invention of the camera, dating back as far as the mid-19th century, although it was not until the end of that century, with the Crimean War (1853-56), that war photographs were specifically used in journalism to inform the public. War photographers and journalists are protected by international conventions, but it remains a potentially lethal profession.

Themes

We live in an age of *"Fake News"*. Technology has enabled anyone to post images or reports and have them widely published, without checks on their authority or authenticity. We can no longer blindly trust what we view or read. This makes this poem and its themes particularly relevant. One central issue with photo-journalism, and a theme of the poem, is **the tension between representation and selection** and hence between **truth and reality.** On the one hand, war photographers wish to capture a realistic, documentary, account of the conflict. On the other, they are bound to newspapers who wish to sell to the public. This results in both photographers and newspaper editors selecting, and potentially manipulating, the images captured. For example, newspaper editors may regard images as too graphic for the general public and censor publication, as in the First World War, when images of soldiers who suffered horrific injuries were suppressed, so as not to demoralise the families back at home. On the other hand, a single powerful image can lead to a global campaign to end a conflict, as during the Vietnam War (1955-1975), when a photograph of a young Vietnamese girl running naked and screaming down a road, having been hit by napalm, was published.[27] Tennyson in *"The Charge of the Light Brigade"* self-censored his original poem to satisfy the public and fulfil his duties as poet laureate. In *"Belfast Confetti"*, Carson struggles to capture the realities of what he is seeing, this time in words rather than pictures. In *"What Were They Like?"*, Levertov adopts the persona of a war correspondent to document the experiences of survivors.

The poem also explores the **effect of conflict on non-combatants** – people who are not directly involved in the fighting. Although they may appear to be detached from their subject matter, war photographers, journalists and other commentators are inevitably affected by their experiences. Nick Ut, the photographer of the little girl, made sure she was taken

---

[27] An interview with the photographer can be found here: https://www.nbcnews.com/video/how-nick-ut-s-photo-napalm-girl-changed-the-vietnam-war-908256835749

to hospital, and was reunited with her years after the war. Satyamurti considers the dilemma between reportage and engagement with the conflict, giving away the photographer's emotional response in the reference to a *"bloodstain on a wall"*. Even Tennyson, in *"The Charge of the Light Brigade"*, which is an unashamedly partisan view of the War, refers to a *"blunder"*. Ciaran Carson in *"Belfast Confetti"* records the reactions of a man who is an innocent bystander, and yet is profoundly affected by the conflict raging around him, as is the survivor interviewed in *"What Were They Like?"*.

Form, structure and language

The poem is a *dramatic monologue*, the speaker a war photographer who is reflecting on the dilemmas he/she faces in her profession. The poem is written in *free verse*, the line breaks guiding the reader through the thoughts of the speaker as she attempts to reconcile her profession with her morals.

The **first stanza** sets out the debate, which is paradoxical: irrespective of what the photographer selects to photograph and place within the *"frame"* (the word taken from picture framing), the viewer can be "reassured" that all is right with the world. The frame is *"flexible"* because the viewer reads what he wants into the image. So, if what you are looking at is painful (*"tragic, absurd"*) you can reassure yourself that it has been deliberately "sought out" by the photographer and that everything outside his frame is "normal". Conversely, if what you see in the image is happy (*"lifts* *the heart"*), the selection can be a reassuring representation of how life is in general.

Notice how this rather complex idea is carefully spelled out to the reader by breaking up the syntax of the single sentence across the lines, indicated by the verbs: *"is flexible/can think/people eat/I seek out/to make."* This patterning continues with the next sentence: *"Or if...lifts/can convince/this is how"*.

Stanza two is connected to the previous stanza by running this sentence across, as indicated by the hyphen, as she moves on to gives us examples of the proposition she has made in stanza one. The first example illustrates her point that images that *"lift the heart"* are representative of the world in general. She has captured an image of girls enjoying themselves at the Ascot races, a meeting which is notorious for attracting the wealthy, upper-classes. *"Peach"* is a reference to their skin - soft, faintly downy and blushed pink; they are made golden by the sunlight; they wear silk, an expensive fabric which they can afford to "crumple" by rolling on the grass; expensive champagne is their drink of choice. It is an image of hedonistic (carefree, selfish) pleasure.

Stanza three again opens with a hyphen, linking it to the ideas in stanza one, here giving an example of the other type of image that the photographer captures. This duplicated structure of the two stanzas mimics the idea of the two opposing, but equal, images. The description of the second image reveals that the idea in the first stanza has been prompted by a recent assignment in a war-zone. The anonymity and universality of war is shown by the unnamed street ("*some*"), whilst the struggle of the child is shown in "*staggering/thrust/weight*". The child sees that she is being photographed and momentarily pauses; it is the moment the photographer captures by pressing the shutter.

In **stanza four**, this moment of stillness is shattered by "*the first bomb of the morning*" which suggests that this is a prolonged conflict in which the dropping bombs are an expected, regular occurrence. The child is terrified, as indicated by the "*dark scream*" from a mouth which is physically too small, it seems, to be able to produce such a scream but which also, metaphorically, is too young to have to. The child drops the baby, which has now become a "*burden*", and runs in an instinctive effort to survive. What happens to the baby we are not told – it is something which happens outside the "frame" of the photographer and, as the *ellipsis* suggests, ceases to exist. We may be reminded of it, however, in the later "*bloodstain*" on the wall.

Stanza five shows the image that has been captured, the newspaper's manipulation of it and the reaction of the photographer to the resulting distortion of the "truth". The picture has captured the fraction of a second between the child noticing the photographer, reacting to her picture being taken with an "*almost smile*" and the dropping of the bomb which causes her to flee in terror. The caption neatly "frames" the image to give it a positive spin, depicting the child as a caring "*mother*", showing her "indomitable spirit"; of *"triumph"* rather than the reality of a terrified abandonment of the child and a retreat.

The photographer reflects that, unlike the images framed for her photographs, which can manipulate the viewer's response, the realities of joy and sorrow - *"heaven and hell"* – are far less easy to capture. They blur into one another and defy definition – *"arbitrary"* – being as formless as a *"blood stain"*. The blood stain is also anonymous – it could be friend or foe.

We are perhaps reminded of Wordsworth's *"moments in time"* which come to define our understanding of life. Wordsworth struggles with understanding what the *"huge peak, black and huge"* means, although he recognises it as a *"moment in time"* that has significance. Similarly, the war photographer acknowledges that interpreting what has happened as *"heaven or hell"* is difficult – *"untidy"*.

Belfast Confetti – Ciaran Carson

Context

Ciaran Carson is an Irish writer and winner of several prestigious poetry prizes. He grew up on Raglan Street in the Falls Road area of Belfast and still lives in the city. Much of the Falls Road area, where this poem is set, was built during the late 19th century and the streets are named after episodes in the Crimean War, the setting for Tennyson's poem *"The Charge of the Light Brigade"*. Balaclava, Inkerman and Odessa were scenes of conflict and Raglan was commander of the troops sent to the Crimea. In themselves, these street names are a reminder of the long-lasting effects of conflict.

The poem was written in the late 1980s during the height of the Troubles in Northern Ireland, which he experienced. This was an extended period of conflict between Republicans from the south and the Unionists of the north which spilled over into terrorist activity on the mainland of Britain. The conflict was resolved in 1998, under the Labour Government of Tony Blair through the Good Friday agreement, which was approved by the Irish people in two referenda.

During the Troubles (1969-1997), Northern Ireland was effectively under military rule by the British Army, supported by The Royal Ulster Constabulary, the police force of Northern Ireland, with checkpoints at the border with the south and armed patrols on the streets of Belfast. The main opposition were members of the Independent Republican Army (IRA) and the Irish

National Liberation Army (INLA). The Army and the RUC, although ostensibly neutral and protecting all members of the public in Northern Ireland, were viewed with hostility by the Catholic minority and frequently came under attack by rioters, as in this poem.

Themes

As in *"War-Photographer"* and *"What Were They Like?"*, the poem considers the **effect of conflict on the non-combatant**, in this case a writer. The use of the *lexis* of writing to describe the actions of the rioters and his own confused reactions also **explores the difficulty of accurately representing the reality** of conflict. Just as the *"War Photographer"* struggles to capture an image which tells the truth with a camera, so Carson attempts to represent what he sees and hears with the tools of his trade – words.

Form, structure and language

It is always risky to base comments on structure on the layout of poems on the page, as this poem appears in a variety of printed forms depending on how it has been typeset[28]. The lines should be read to include the shorter sections – where the long lines break varies from version to version. So the first line reads from: *"Suddenly..."* to *"...exclamation marks"* and the second from *"Nuts,..."* to *"...explosion"* and so on. Whilst it appears to be in a free-flowing form, each of these long

---

[28] See the *"Note on typography"* at the beginning of the Guide

lines has roughly ten stressed beats, which makes it less disjointed than it appears on the page. It would, therefor, be risky to draw any conclusions from the layout as presented in this printed version.

The poem is split into two stanzas – the first recording a clash between rioters and the *"riot squad"* of the RUC, the second the disjointed, panicked thoughts of a man caught up in it – either real or imagined. The punctuation of the second stanza also contributes to the atmosphere of chaos, as the reader hears the speaker's panicked thoughts as he tries to escape the confusion of the confrontation.

"Belfast Confetti" is the street name given to the various missiles thrown at the soldiers and police by the rioters, such as *"Nuts, bolts, nails, car-keys"* but Carson intersperses these with the *lexis* of typesetting – *"exclamation marks"*, *"A fount of broken type"* - to show how his world as a writer has been disrupted by the civil war on the streets and how he struggles to express what is happening. The sounds of the riot on the street become merged with the thoughts of the writer as he tries to make sense of the confusion.

The explosion that follows the hail of missiles *"raining"* down on the soldiers is described as an *"asterisk"* on a map of the streets – a sudden starburst *. The stutter of machine-gun fire is represented by a *"hyphen"* – a break in a line. His attempts to think straight are hindered by *"dead ends"*, the *"stops and colons"* stopping him like the roadblocks set up around the riot zone.

In **stanza two**, he imagines himself on the streets of Belfast, running from the soldiers. He names the streets, as they recall another conflict. Although these streets are familiar to him (he has lived there all his life), he cannot find a way through; there are blockages (*"punctuated"*) at every turn. As he becomes hemmed in, he sees the approaching armoured vehicles of the riot police – a tank manned by police in riot gear. What follows are questions, ostensibly asked by the police. However, the questions seem to come not from an external source, but from inside his own head. What is his place in this conflict and how can he escape it? The questions come like a hail of bullets – a *"fusillade"*.

The para-rhyme of *"rioter"* and *"writer"* takes on new significance. Although not a "rioter" on the streets of Belfast, as a "writer", Carson can make his own protest through his poetry and stories.

The Class Game – Mary Casey

Context

There are two poets called Mary Casey; on-line resources variously attribute this poem to a writer from Dorset who died in 1989 and whose work was published posthumously, and a woman from Liverpool whose only published works were in a local literary magazine called "*Voices*". The poem is by the latter, who is described in the Spring 1979 Issue 19 of the magazine as "*a housewife from Cantril Farm overspill estate, Liverpool.*"[29]

During the 1960s, the Beatles and the Liverpool Sound placed the city at the centre of global popular culture. However, in common with other major industrial centres in the north of England, Liverpool suffered significant social and economic deprivation during the 1970s and 1980s as the manufacturing and shipping base on which it relied was gradually eroded. The introduction of containerised shipping, in particular, led to massive job losses and by 1982, unemployment was at 17%. Liverpool also became infamous in 1981 for the racially charged Toxteth Riots in which rioters protested police treatment of black residents. The Cantrill Estate, built to take residents from the centre of Liverpool after the war, is remembered by early residents as initially a pleasant neighbourhood. However, by the early 1980s

---

[29] A copy of the magazine can be found here: http://www.mancvoices.co.uk/issue_19.htm

it was characterised by high unemployment, social deprivation and crime.

Themes

In *"The Class Game"*, Casey challenges the reader's assumptions about her social class based on her *dialect*, where she lives and the occupations of her family. She sees the habit of trying to guess a person's class as a *"Game"* people play. Her anger at being type-cast is shared by Zephaniah's *"No Problem"*, and Agard's *"Half-caste"* which also challenge the **stereotyping of people to demean them** and the **conflict in society** which this creates.

Form, structure and language

Contrary to initial impressions, this is a highly-crafted and sophisticated poem. Even the title is a pun on "Class War", and the idea of "war games", a metaphor used by many poets. It is a *monologue* written in a single stanza of *rhyming couplets* in *trochaic tetrametres*[30], except for three lines towards the end which are in *trimetres*, designed to speed up the rhythm and add to the defiant tone. This makes it highly structured and classic in form, or *"posh"*, its crafting challenging the assumption that people who speak in a *dialect* are uneducated. The question *"How can you tell?"* introduces each example of class discrimination

---

[30] Four beats of mainly *trochaic* metric feet – **heavy**/light, or **TUM**-ti

and acts as a refrain, suggesting her frustration at being put in a category.

Casey uses accent, *dialect* words and non-standard grammar to reproduce the sound of the Liverpudlian accent, to create a humorous, mocking tone directed at her "middle-class" reader. Both Agard and Zephaniah adopt a similarly self-conscious *dialect* to convey their message.

The poem opens with a challenge to the reader in the form of a *rhetorical question*, defying them to define her class from the way she speaks. This use of *rhetorical questions* can be compared with those in Levertov's poem *"What were they like?"* which similarly answers them as well as asks. Casey claims that she too can speak in Received Pronunciation, or *"posh"*, if she puts an *"Olly"* in her mouth – a *dialect* word for a marble. This would force her to round her vowels and speak more nasally, characteristic of Received Pronunciation (RP) or Southern accent. She could also wear an *"'at"* (hat) rather than the headscarf that is stereotypical of a working-class woman, even if her clothes are second-hand, hiding her "class". She asks why her reader *"winces"*, showing disapproval, when she uses the familiar forms of "Goodbye" (*"Tara"*) and *"Ma"* instead of *"Mummy"*, when the meaning and feeling behind the words, which is what matters, are the same.

The rhetorical question is repeated to introduce the idea of judgements on class being made based on where you live. She lives in a *"corpy"* or Council House (social housing) rather than a semi-detached house out in the prettier suburbs of the Wirral, from which the residents commute into Liverpool to work, rather than working close to home and walking. The suggestion that she might have dropped her "*unemployment card*" on their "*patio*" is ironic. She would be unlikely to be invited to sit on their patio – which is the "posh" word for her "*backyard*".

In the next section, she asks if her class can be told from a label she wears, the crudity of "*bum*" raising the emotional tone to one of anger, as it is designed to shock. "*Stained with toil*" and the "*lily-white*" are references to the line in the Bible "*Behold the lilies of the field; they toil not neither do they spin*". These literary references are at odds with the vernacular of the previous line, as if taunting her reader that she, too, can show off her literary credentials. In the next lines she reverts to the *vernacular*, the language of speech, mocking the habit of tea-drinkers and their use of *euphemisms* for words for our common bodily functions: "*toilet/bog", "pee*".

The last section opens rhetorically asking why the listener should care about her class, or do they see it as an affront to them - something which makes them uncomfortable, like a "*sour plum*" stuck in their throats? With an exclamatory "*Well, Mate,*" Casey dispenses with the questions and emphatically sets out her position, speeding up the rhythm by switching to *trimetres (*three stresses) in the final lines to give further emphasis. "*Wet nelly*" is a Lancashire form of a moist, fruit cake called a Nelson cake. Casey defiantly states who and what she is, unashamedly using her *dialect*. She dispenses with all pretence, declaring her pride in who she is.

The whole poem is, in itself, a "conflict", or contradiction, between the subject matter, which is about making judgements based on class, and the language, form and structure of the poem. Whilst professing to be written by a woman from the working class, who does not speak "posh" but rather in *dialect*, she actually writes in standard English, although she sprinkles *dialect* throughout, and uses a sophisticated metric structure. This makes the identity of the poet something of a mystery and proves the point that making judgements based on how you speak is risky.

Poppies – Jane Weir

Context

This poem was written as a contribution to a collection, called *"Exit Wounds"*, commissioned by Carol Ann Duffy, the current Poet Laureate, and printed in *The Guardian* newspaper in 2009, just after Duffy took up her office. At the time, British troops were engaged in Afghanistan, where they had been since 2001, following the USA's declaration of war after the attack on the Twin Towers in New York on *9/11*. Duffy commented:

With the official inquiry into Iraq imminent and the war in Afghanistan returning dead teenagers to the streets of Wootton Bassett, I invited a range of my fellow poets to bear witness, each in their own way, to these matters of war.[31]

Weir's intention in writing the poem can be found in an interview she gave in 2010 here:
http://www.sheerpoetry.co.uk/gcse/jane-weir/poppies-jane-weir-interviewed-by-luca-brancati

The title *"Poppies"* inevitably recalls the First World War. Poppies prefer land which is regularly tilled for crop planting and, before the war, they grew in abundance in Flanders, where much of the War was fought. The constant upheaval to the land caused by shelling suited them well and they flourished even in

---

[31] https://www.theguardian.com/books/2009/jul/25/war-poetry-carol-ann-duffy

the midst of the destruction. A famous poem of the War, by the Canadian John McCrae, begins:

*"In Flanders field the poppies blow
Between the crosses, row on row"*

The poppy was adopted by the Royal British Legion in 1921 as its symbol of Remembrance for its fundraising efforts.

Commentaries on Weir's poem show considerable confusion about the sequence of events, what exactly is happening, and when. Some commentators set the poem after the son has died, equating the farewell at the beginning with the mother seeing her son off to war and her visit to the cemetery as an act of remembrance that takes place after his death. But this cannot be right – the language and imagery does not support the idea of the boy, whom she bids farewell in the opening lines, being a young soldier. He is clearly a young child going off to, possibly, secondary school. There is no shift in time; the events take place in a single morning. Rather, the poem is an *analogy*[32] between bidding a son goodbye as he goes off to school and saying goodbye to a son going to war. This interpretation is supported by Weir herself in the interview.

Jane Weir is a textile designer and draws on the *semantic field* [33]of textiles for much of her imagery. She

---

[32] An *analogy* is a comparison for illustrative purposes
[33] A *semantic field* is the use of words all associated with a particular topic.

has two sons and acknowledges having the feelings expressed in the poem. The setting is based on the graveyard of the church where she lives and where she would walk with her sons when they were young.

Themes

The overwhelming emotion in the poem is a feeling of **Loss,** and Weir explores this feeling through the relationship between a mother and her young son. The poem makes an *analogy* between the feelings of loss felt by a mother who parts from her son as he goes off to school, and as he grows up and away from her, with those of a mother who loses her son to war. Whether this is a valid comparison, convincingly expressed through the poetry, is a matter of opinion. It is perhaps best to regard it as an account of an actual happening which can stand alone, whilst enabling the reader to draw wider inferences from it on the nature of loss in times of war and more generally.

Weir is reflecting on **the effect of conflict on the individual.** Weir has said that she was *"angry and frustrated at the apathy, or what I perceived as 'voicelessness' and ability to be heard or get any kind of justice."* Like in *"War Photographer"* and *"What Were They Like?"*, the person affected is not a soldier, but a civilian. It also has clear similarities with Clarke's *"Catrin"* in exploring the **conflict between a mother and child** as the child seeks a greater independence in adolescence.

Form, structure and language

The poem is a *monologue* written in *free verse*. The use of the imagery of textiles, coupled with Weir's own testimony, identifies the speaker with the poet, Jane Weir, as does her own commentary on it[34]. The tone of the whole is meditative and melancholy, with long lines like a prose poem.

The first stanza sets the poem firmly in time – it is *"three days"* before the commemoration of the end of the First World War and all other wars that followed, when poppies are sold for charity and decorate war-graves. The *"you"* of line 3 is not identified, but the use of the words *"lapel"*, *"bias binding"* and *"blazer"* all suggest that the person is wearing a school blazer, not a uniform jacket, which has neither lapels, nor bias binding (the ribbon sewn around the edges of jackets to protect them from wear) and is not called a *blazer*[35]. However, the words used to describe the act of pinning on the paper poppy are in the *semantic field* of conflict – *"spasms"* as of pain, *"red"* suggesting blood, *"blockade"* as in a military exercise, developing the *analogy*.

In stanza two, the suggestion that this is a child, not an adult about to go to war, is stronger. The actions of the mother, like the pinning of the poppy, are nurturing and over-protective. The mother cleans the cat hairs off his

---

[34] https://www.youtube.com/watch?v=r8QIcYdJPG0
[35] A *regimental blazer*, worn on formal occasions, does have lapels – but a soldier going to war would not be wearing one.

blazer; interferes with his collar which he has (perhaps defiantly?) turned up; at least she resists infantilising him by "*play[ing] at being Eskimos*" or mussing his hair. But the sense of the child beginning to break free of this parental (s)mothering is there, in the "*upturned*" collar and the "*gelled blackthorns of [his] hair*". "*Blackthorns*" are bushes which have sharp thorns on them, signifying "do not touch", as the child resists his mother's control. Her feelings as she is about to wave her son off to school are complex. Weir uses another war image to show that the mother doesn't want her son to see that she is upset – she "*steels*" her face, turns it hard and expressionless. She finds herself unable to express her feelings in words, using imagery from textiles to show how her words become useless, like soft, formless, fabric. The "*melting*" is possibly a reference to her "*steel*" face revealing her true feelings, rather than her words.

In the **third stanza**, she rallies ("*was brave*") as she lets the child out. The image of the "*treasure chest*" again suggests youthful excitement. It is an image from adventures in childhood – from the book "*Treasure Island*" with its pirates and treasure maps. The child bounds away, made drunk with the excitement of being set free – again, a youthful image not in keeping with the suggestions that this is a man going off to war. It expresses carefree, joyous excitement without any backward glance or regret.

The mother then goes into the child's bedroom. At this point, the *literal* (the real mother in a real bedroom with a bird in a cage) and the *analogous* become

83

confusingly separated. It is hard to believe that a child actually keeps a song bird in a cage, so this must be a *symbol* for allowing the child (the *"song bird"*) free of maternal control. Similarly, with the dove and the pear tree; both images are too trite (and unlikely) to be real – and shouldn't it be a partridge in a pear tree? The dove is (too?) obviously a symbol of peace. This imagery does not really work, because an analogy or symbol should illuminate the subject, adding to our understanding, rather than detracting.

Later that day, the mother follows the real (or symbolic) dove up to the cemetery by the church to stand by the war memorial. Her feelings of sorrow and loss are made physically evident by a "knot" in her stomach, which she again describes using the imagery of textiles, listing various types of stitching: *"tucks /darts /pleats"*, which are all used to gather together material. She has given no thought to her own comfort. She has left her coat, hat and gloves, her guards against the weather, and, by *analogy,* against her grief, behind. These are described in military language as *"reinforcements"*, guarding her against the enemy of her sorrow.

The last stanza sees the mother reaching the war memorial on the hill, examining the names carved in it, and leaning against it, *"like a wishbone"*. A *"wishbone"* is a bone like an inverted "Y", joined at the top, which forms part of the collarbone of a bird. Traditionally, the wishbone of edible birds, like turkeys, is "pulled" between two people, each grasping one side. When the bone snaps in two, the person left holding the small, joining bone at the top is the "winner" and can make a wish. She is likening herself to one half of the wishbone after it has been "pulled" apart, as she has been from her son, and cannot stand upright on her own, but has to lean against the memorial. This idea is reinforced as she watches the dove fly by, now an image of her son "*pull[ing] freely*" away from her, his separation from her further signified by the use of "*ornamental*" – the *stitch* now has no purpose, it cannot hold them together. As she stands there, she hopes to hear her son's voice carried up from the school playground to her on the wind, as a longed-for link between them, and a way of "*catching*" him back, as if he were a dropped "*stitch*". By *analogy*, the mother left behind after a son has gone to war might hope to receive a telegram or letter from the son who has been deployed to the front line, the "*playground*" being an *analogy* for the field of battle. This *analogy* between a school playground and a battlefield most famously occurs in the poem "*Vitaï Lampada*" by Henry Newbolt (1862-1938), in which cricket, played at his public school, was likened to a battle.

No Problem – Benjamin Zephaniah

Context

Benjamin Zephaniah was born in Birmingham to parents from the Caribbean. He describes himself as *"Poet, writer, lyricist, musician and naughty boy."* He has just published (May 2018) his autobiography. Zephaniah has a blog which gives details of his life that can be found here: https://benjaminzephaniah.com.

His poetry explores the experience of black people living in Britain, charting the politics of race from the open discrimination of the 1970s through to the present. *"No Problem"* was written in 1996, twenty years after the passing of the Race Relations act of 1976 which itself replaced the first act of 1965. The Acts were consolidated in 2010. In a recent interview with The Observer newspaper, Zephaniah expressed his pessimism at the progress of race relations in Britain today: *"I feel we've taken so many steps backwards and so quickly. I used to say that, when I get to 60, it's not going to be a perfect world, but it's going to be so cool, I can relax, I can turn into a Rastafarian comedian. No way, I've got to be the angry black poet again."*

Themes

The poem has the theme of **stereotyping causing conflict between people** in common with Agard's *"Half-caste"* and Casey's *"The Class Game"*. Zephaniah also uses *dialect* to express his exasperation at the categorisation of black, young, people as *"the problem"*, when *"the problem"* lies in the eye of the, predominantly white, beholder. Like Casey and Agard, he gives examples of the absurdity of regarding people as a "type", and discriminating against them as a result, with negative outcomes. The theme of **racial discrimination** also aligns the poem with Levertov's *"What Were They Like?"*

Form, language and structure

The poem is a *monologue,* notable for its short lines which echo the speech rhythms and *dialect* of British Jamaicans. It has a strong rhythm, which aligns it with *dub poetry*[36], designed to be chanted, each line having three or four stressed beats. As in *"The Class Game"* and *"Half-caste"*, much use is made of repetition, each recurrence of the refrain sounding more absurd as the poem progresses. The regular rhythm is supported by a regular rhyme scheme, with each alternate line rhyming: *"brunt/stunts", "academic/athletic"*. As in Casey's poem, this structure is an ironic comment on the assumptions made about people who do not fit the traditional idea of a "poet".

The poem is split into two stanzas, the first made up of *quatrains,* introduced by the question of the refrain, in which the poet gives his example of stereotyping. The second stanza reflects on his experience and turns the tables on his white readership.

---

[36] *Dub poetry* developed in the West Indies (Caribbean) out of dub reggae music (spoken word over heavy, mellow and often psychedelic sounds). (*TES*)

The first *quatrain* recaps on experiences as a child, when the speaker was bullied at school for being black. He then comments on the stereotyping of black boys as *"athletic"* rather than *"academic"*, closing off opportunities for higher education. *"Branding"* means to mark out, but it is also a reference to the enslavement of black Africans, who were branded to show ownership by their white masters. *"On the run"* is a contrastingly humorous reference to running from trouble. Zephaniah is dyslexic and was expelled from school at 14. He resorted to petty theft and was sent to borstal, a school for troublesome children. Very little attention was paid to children with special educational needs in the 1960s and 70s and children who struggled academically were often written off, leaving school with few qualifications and fewer prospects of gainful employment, circumstances which underlie Casey's poem as well. Being able to dance is another stereotype of black people, and Zephaniah comments on the lack of *"chances"* for these children by asserting that he could have answered academic questions as well (*"versatile"*) on subjects such as Geography, given the chance. Instead he was *"pigeon-holed*[37]*"* by pre-conceived notions of his ability.

The **second stanza** reflects on the effect of these prejudices as he grows older, although he claims that he bears no ill-will. He reasserts that *"black is not the*

---

[37] *"pigeon-hole"* is a reference to the holes in dovecotes, in which doves and pigeons were kept as a food source in medieval times.

problem", urging England, the *"mother-country"* to finally understand that the problem lies with her. England was called the *"mother-country"* during the days of Empire, as it viewed itself, and encouraged others to think of it, as a benevolent carer for the peoples of the Empire. The epithet was used to encourage people of the Windrush generation in the 1950s and 60s to come to England to work, filling the vacancies left by the war and post-war regeneration. His final, ironic statement plays on the defence made by white people when they claim not to be racially prejudiced. Not only does Zephaniah not bear a grudge, he claims, but his remarks are not, of course, directed at **all** white people. White people claim some of their best friends are black, as if befriending an individual excuses white society's attitude towards the black community as a whole. The irony is that it is predominantly white people who have established the social, economic and political frameworks in which these prejudices flourish, and so they do, in fact, bear collective responsibility for how black people are treated.

What Were They Like? – Denise Levertov

Context

Born in England in 1923 to Welsh and Russian-Jewish parents, Denise Levertov emigrated to the United States as a young woman when she married an American writer. She became involved in social and political change movements, including opposition to the Vietnam War, which this poem, written in 1966, is about. It is, in effect, a *protest poem*, such as those produced by singers and poets in the 1960s, like Bob Dylan, Woody Guthrie and Joan Baez.

The war started in 1959 and ended in 1975, in a stalemate between the USA and the communist forces, the Viet Cong. Vietnam was a former French Colony and was partitioned between North Vietnam (which was Communist under its leader, Ho Chi Minh) and South Vietnam, (led by the American supported President Diem) following the departure of the French in 1950s. Afraid of the spread of Communism in SE Asia, and the growing insurgence of Communists in the South (Viet Cong), the US increased its involvement. Between 1965 and 1968, the US ran bombing attacks in North Vietnam and landed ground troops. This was the era of the infamous remark attributed to the Chief of Staff of the US Airforce: "*We're going to bomb them into the Stone Age*". US warfare included bombing with the use of *defoliants,* such as Agent Orange, which caused subsequent defects in children born after the war and *napalm*, a sticky, incendiary material. In response, the Viet Cong moved to *guerilla* warfare, considerably complicating the course of the war as the *guerillas* hid amongst civilians, who became targets for the US warplanes and ground troops. Public support in the US declined rapidly through the late 60s with global anti-war protests. The US withdrew between 1974 – 1975. Soon after, Saigon fell to the Northern army and the Socialist Republic of Vietnam was founded.

Themes

The poem is a protest poem but also *an elegy*, mourning the death of the civilians killed in the Vietnam war and the loss of their traditional way of life. The poem re-imagines the aftermath of war and its **effect on the civilian population**. In this, Levertov's poem can be compared to *"War Photographer"*, *"Belfast Confetti"* or *"Poppies"*. The poem explores how conflict destroys, not just bodies and buildings, but the cultural identity, and the future, of the non-combatants, leaving wounds that cannot be healed.

Form, structure and language

The poem is framed as an interview between a war correspondent, or reporter, and a survivor of the conflict, in a series of structured questions and answers. Although this format might suggest a clinical and unemotional response to the suffering, the verbal linking of the questions and answers creates a strong sense of empathy with the survivor.

Each line is roughly the same length, with four stresses, although the rhythm is hard to detect owing to the frequent use of *enjambment* (where the sense of the line is carried over to the next) as in: *"Did they hold ceremonies/ to reverence the opening of buds?"* This gives it a conversational tone at odds with the formal structure.

The first stanza is structured as a numbered series of questions, as if from an interviewer, about the way the Vietnamese lived their lives before the war, their customs and ceremonies. **Question 1** refers to the characteristic stone lanterns of the region that are set in gardens and along pathways. **Question 2** recalls ceremonies to celebrate the coming of spring. **Question 3** suggests their social gatherings with friends and family. **Question 4** asks about the ornamentation of their bodies and clothes, using traditional materials. **Question 5** enquires about their oral culture - how they celebrate their past in legends and myths. **Question 6** suggests that for them their oral culture was strong, with little difference between everyday speaking and singing.

The second stanza gives the corresponding numbered responses by the survivor. The responses are linked to the questions by the repetition of words in the questions, which gives the poem its own unique structure. Each answer subtly changes the tone of the question, from neutral to emotionally charged, reflecting the trauma of the aftermath of the conflict. **Answer 1** picks up on *"lanterns of stone"*, suggestive of light, with *"light hearts turned to stone"*, shifting the question from the physical consequences to the emotional. Whether they had stone lanterns appears an irrelevance now – they cannot remember in these dark days. **Answer 2** links the idea of celebrating spring with the flowering of *"blossom"*, but then goes on to mourn the death of the people's own *"buds"*, their children or offspring. **Answer 3** gives a terse response to the idea of laughter. People were burned with Napalm in the bombing; there is no laughter now. **Answer 4** suggests that their past life is only a dream and that decorations are for when you are feeling happy and content and such things have been destroyed in the bombing. *"The bones"* refers to both the bone ornaments and the bones of the victims. **Answer 5** shows how their past, contained in their shared oral history, has been shattered by the war. In times of peace, there were opportunities in the quiet moments to hand down stories across the generations. But that peaceful life, and the continuity that it promised, has been *"smashed"* by the bombs, just like the quiet, reflecting waters of the rice paddies in which they worked. There was no longer time to tell stories – all they could do was *"scream"* in terror. **Answer 6** replies that faint echoes of their speaking can still be heard. The survivor likens their voices to *"moths in moonlight"*, the *alliteration* adding to the delicacy of the image, which suggests fragility and impermanence, easily destroyed. There are few people left now who can speak of the sound of their voices, which have been silenced in death.

Links, Connections, Comparisons & Tackling the Unseen Poem

The exam question (the "task")

The exam question will give you a *"theme"* to discuss as a guide to which aspects of the poem(s) they want you to focus on. They will probably use the word *"Compare"*. Where possible, links and connections should be made to each poem throughout the essay, alternating between the two, for the highest marks. The examiners are less keen on one analysis followed by another, unless there is clear cross-referencing and/or there is a clearly comparative paragraph at the beginning and at the end.

What is happening in the poem?

The first task is to understand *"What is happening in the poem?"* Unless you understand this, your analysis will be meaningless. Make sure you understand what the story, incident, event or imaginative idea is that has prompted the poet to write the poem. No poem exists in a vacuum – there is always a reason for writing it. Find that reason – the inspiration which leads to the poem.

The first "link or connection" to be made is to summarise, briefly, the "story" of each poem **and how this relates to the theme of the question.** This is the first response to *"How"* the poet has approached his subject. It is the framework around which he hangs his ideas. It is suggested that you do this in your first paragraph. It also reassures the Examiner that your analysis is not starting from an erroneous base. **Make** the "story" the first point of comparison between the texts.

What is the relevant context within which the whole poem is written?

Make any immediate comparisons of "**context**". Are the poems addressing the same themes but within **a different time-frame** (past/present, for example)? Is there any relevance of the theme to our **experience today which is different to theirs**? Are the poets writing in a particular **literary tradition**? What do you know about **the poets' lives** that is relevant and may be a cause for writing the poems? Are there any **specific events** that the poems are referring to?

Ensure that you always relate context back to the question. They do not want, for example, a history of Romantic poetry – but they do want you to show that you understand their **predominant concerns and styles** and **how this is reflected** in the poetry.

As you discuss **form, structure and language**, refer to any relevant **contextual factors that affect the choice of these elements**. For example, the use of classical or religious imagery reflecting a literary tradition or societal norms; use of language forms, such as *dialect*, that are used to convey the message of the poem.

Form, Structure and Language

A poem may have many ideas in it. Your task is to explain **how the poet has used form, structure and language to explore the theme which is the focus of the question.** Below are some of the features of the poems that you can choose to explore, both when making links, connections and comparisons between the prescribed poem and one other from the *Anthology*, AND when linking the two Unseen poems.

Remember that the highest marks are given when the analysis of form, structure and language is related to meaning and to the theme under discussion. Fewer marks are given for merely identifying techniques in isolation from meaning. The commentaries on the poems show you how to do this.

It is important that you use *"examples"* (quotes) to illustrate your argument. Never make a comment about how the poet has approached his subject without an example to illustrate. You should also **never use a quote without then going on to talk about the quote** itself, analysing any structural or language features in depth and **relating this to the writer's intention**. This ensures that you are covering the assessment objective AO2 – *"showing a critical understanding of the writer's craft."* However, comments like *"paint a picture in your mind"* or *"make the reader feel sorry for..."* are too general to gain credit at the higher levels. You need to be specific about why a writer has chosen a language or structural feature.

Theme	The question will focus on a theme. Some key themes have been identified in the commentary on the texts. Choose poems which can be linked thematically as a first choice for linking, connecting and comparing. Trying to link poems "because you know them" is not a good plan.
Context	Is there a historical /biographical /literary /political/ social-economic background that is relevant to the text and the way it is written? **How does the context of the text relate to the meaning of the text and help us to understand it?**
Narrative Voice	Who is speaking in the poem? Is it the poet, or is he speaking through someone else? Is there more than one *voice*? The narrative voice is the person who is speaking in the poem. It may be the poet (many of the poems are autobiographical) or a *persona* – an imagined speaker, as in a *dramatic monologue*. Or it may be the poet simply talking to us about an idea that he/she wishes to explore. **What does the choice of narrative voice tell us about the poet's approach to his theme or about the theme itself?**

Form	Is the poem written in a named poetic form, such as *sonnet, ode, elegy, ballad*? **What does the choice of form tell you about the subject matter or the attitude of the poet?**
Structure	How many lines are there in a stanza? How is the story arranged around these lines? What is the subject matter of each stanza? In what order has the story or happening been told to us? Are there shifts in time or place? Is there a regular rhythm? If so, what is this rhythm? Is there a regular rhyme scheme? Are *full rhymes, half-rhymes* and *eye-rhymes* used? Are the lines *end-stopped* – does the meaning follow the rhyme and complete at the end of each rhymed line? Does the poet use *enjambment* and *caesura* to vary the pace of the line and create a looser structure within a rigid one? What does this say about the subject matter or the poet's attitude to his subject? Is it in free verse, with no discernible regular rhyme or rhythm? How has the poet chosen where to end the lines? **How does the choice and use of structure relate to meaning and what is the effect on the reader?**

Language	Is the language formal or informal? Does it sound conversational, confiding, reminiscent, musing, purposeful...? What is the tone? Sorrowful, regretful, angry, puzzled, triumphant...? What is the proportion of *vernacular* (words of common speech) to Latinate (polysyllabic, Latin derivations, "difficult")? Is the language descriptive, factual, plain, colloquial ...? Is the language literal, or does it have many *similes* and *metaphors*, or *personification*? What kinds of *imagery* are used: religious, naturalistic, mechanistic...? Are there particular words used which are unusual? Archaic, *dialect*, slang...? **How does the choice and use of language relate to meaning and what is the effect on the reader?**

A Note on Metre

Rhythm in English Verse

Rhythm in English verse is dependent on the **pattern** and **number** of *stressed* and *unstressed* syllables in a line. This is called *metre*. The name given to the *metric line* depends on **a)** the pattern of *stressed* and *unstressed* beats in the *metric feet* and b) the number of *metric feet* in a line. If the pattern changes in a line, the predominant pattern is used to define it.

Pattern

Each pattern of *stressed* and *unstressed* syllables has its own name. In the examples, the *stressed* syllables (or *beats*, as in music) are highlighted. The symbol "/" divides the line into its *metric feet*.

"Had **he**/ and **I**/ but **met**/
By **some**/ old **an**/cient **inn**"/

Here, there are three *metric feet* in each line, each with the pattern "light/**HEAVY**" or "ti-**TUM**". This makes it a *metric line* of three *iambs* – *iambic trimetre*.

Iamb – unstressed, stressed (ti-**TUM**). "With**in**/ a **rock**/y **cove**/, its **us**/ual **home**..." which is a regular iambic line. It is the most common *foot* found in English poetry. Hardy's line above is *iambic trimetre* – three feet of *iambs*.

Trochee – stressed, unstressed (**TUM**-ti). "**I** was/ **an**gry/ **with** my / **friend**" which is *trochee, trochee trochee,* and an unfinished *trochee* – or catalectic ending.

Spondee – stressed, stressed (**TUM-TUM**). "**No more**;/ and **by**/a **sleep**,/ to **say/** we **end**" which is *spondee, iamb, iamb, iamb, iamb*

Dactyl – stressed, unstressed, unstressed (**TUM**-ti-ti). "**Half** a league, **half** a league" which is *dactyl, dactyl.* Another example of a *dactyl* is in the word *"Liverpool"*

Anapest – unstressed, unstressed, stressed (ti-ti-**TUM**) "*The As**syr**ian des**cend**ed like the **wolf** on the **fold**"*, which is a regular *anapaestic* rhyme.

Amphibrach – unstressed, stressed, unstressed (ti-**TUM**-ti) as in *"to**ma**to/po**ta**to".* This is rarely found.

Counting *metric feet*

In Hardy's lines above, there are three *metric feet.* The number of *metric feet* is given a name derived from Greek metrics, as below:

The numbers of *feet* in a line are called:

Trimetre – 3	Hexametre - 6
Tetrametre - 4	Heptametre - 7
Pentametre – 5	Octametre – 8

A *catalectic* line is one where the last, or first, part of a metric foot is missing. This is most clearly seen in Blake's "*A Poison Tree*":

*I was/ **angry**/ **with** my/ **friend***	*trochaic tetrametre catalectic (or headless iambic tetrametre)*
*I **told**/ my **wrath**,/ my **wrath**/ did **end**.*	*Iambic tetrametre*

Line two has four clear *iambic* feet – ti-**TUM**. However, the first line has three clear *trochaic* feet (**TUM**-ti) – plus an extra stressed syllable at the end (***friend***). This unfinished metric foot is called *catalectic*. If it were finished, it would make a line of *trochaic tetrametre*. However, looked at another way, you could say that it is the FIRST syllable of an *iambic tetrametre* line that is missing, hence *"headless"*:

I /was **an/**gry with/ my **friend**	*headless iambic tetrametre*
I **told**/ my **wrath**,/ my **wrath**/ did **end**	*iambic tetrametre*

Note that the last syllable of the *headless* or *catalectic* line has a long vowel or a dipthong: *friend, foe, tears, smiles*. This also serves to disguise the shortening of the metric line.

Metric Forms or Names (given in order of prevalence)

Iambic pentametre – is the commonest metric form in English and comprises a *metric line* of *five iambic feet*. Variation is given by the use of other *feet*, which can give the verse the sound of natural speech rhythms.

However, the *five foot, iambic pattern* is always underlying.

NOTE: you will hear people describe *iambic pentametre* as containing ten unstressed/stressed *syllables*. This is not the case. **It has nothing to do with the number of syllables** – only the number and type of the *feet*. This example (from Wordsworth's *"Extract..."*) makes this clear:

"The ho**ri**/zon's **bound**,/ a **huge**/ peak, **black**/ and **huge**,/"

There are **eleven** syllables – the extra syllable given by the use of the *anapest* (ti-ti-**TUM**) *"The hori/zons..."* – in an otherwise *iambic pentametre* line.

B*lank verse* is *unrhymed iambic pentametre,* commonly used by Shakespeare, but also by Seamus Heaney and other modern poets who write in a classic tradition..

Iambic tetrametre is four *iambic* beats in a line, as used by Christina Rossetti in *"Cousin Kate"*:

"He **saw**/ you **at** /your **fa**/ther's **gate**"

Tetrametre is also the rhythm of many nursery rhymes. We describe this as "sing-song" as it is common in songs and light verse. The four-beat **iambic tetrametre** line may alternate with a three-beat **iambic trimetre** as in **common** or **ballad metre,** used by Hardy in *"The Man He Killed"*:

"I **shot**/ at **him**/ as **he**/ at **me**,
And **killed**/ him **in**/ his **place**"

As here, this *metre* can be used **ironically** by poets when dealing with a serious subject, so watch out for a deliberate mismatch between the metre and the subject matter to make a point.

End-stopping is where the sense of the line, contained in a clause or sentence, ends at the end of the line, where the *metric line* ends, as in Byron's *"The Destruction..."*

*"And the foam of his gasping lay white on the turf,
And cold as the spray of the rock-beating surf"*

This tends to emphasise the rhyme, making it more insistent, and urgent, in keeping with the topic of the poem – the headlong gallop and then the sudden onslaught of the Angel of Death.

Enjambment is the opposite of *end-stopped*. The sense of the line continues onto the next line, often landing on a stressed beat, to emphasise the first word of the line, and enhance meaning, as here in Clarke's *"Catrin"*. It also propels the verse forwards, making it flow, even if there is a regular rhyme scheme.

"As I stood in a hot, **white**
Room *at the window* **watching**
The people *and cars* **taking**
Turn *at the traffic lights.*

Free verse is a modern form of poetry that has no regular *rhythm* or *rhyme*. This is not to say that makes no use of either. If there were neither rhythm nor rhyme throughout, then one might as well call it prose, divided up into arbitrary lines. *Free verse* frequently uses *enjambment* and *caesura* to guide the reader through the argument and create rhythmic and rhyming effects, as here in *"War Photographer"*, where the idea of manipulating the viewer is split into three, clear grammatical sections:

*"Or if the picture's such as lifts the heart
the firmness of the edges can convince you
this is how things are"*

Printed in Great Britain
by Amazon